MEATLESS COOKING

by
Jean Paré

Dedication

Meatless is marvelous!

Cover Photo

1. Tomato Onion Quiche, page 94
2. Zucchini Cutlets, page 87
3. Tabbouleh, page 112
4. Pasta Primavera, page 145

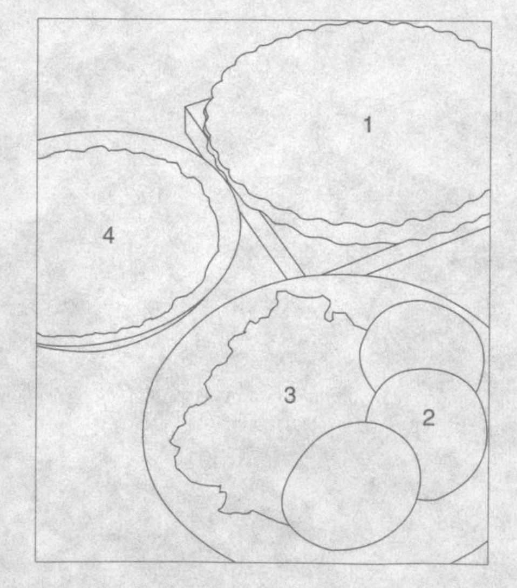

Plate And Bowl Courtesy Of:
Stokes

Napkins Courtesy Of:
La Cache

Fresh Flowers Courtesy Of:
Creations By Design

MEATLESS COOKING

Second Printing April 1997

ISBN 1-895455-23-5

Published and Distributed by
Company's Coming Publishing Limited
Box 8037, Station "F"
Edmonton, Alberta, Canada
T6H 4N9

**Published Simultaneously in
Canada and the United States of America**

Printed In Canada

Company's Coming Cookbooks by Jean Paré

COMPANY'S COMING SERIES
English

- 150 DELICIOUS SQUARES
- CASSEROLES
- MUFFINS & MORE
- SALADS
- APPETIZERS
- DESSERTS
- SOUPS & SANDWICHES
- HOLIDAY ENTERTAINING
- COOKIES
- VEGETABLES
- MAIN COURSES
- PASTA
- CAKES
- BARBECUES
- DINNERS OF THE WORLD
- LUNCHES
- PIES
- LIGHT RECIPES
- MICROWAVE COOKING
- PRESERVES
- LIGHT CASSEROLES
- CHICKEN, ETC.
- KIDS COOKING
- FISH & SEAFOOD
- BREADS
- MEATLESS COOKING
- COOKING FOR TWO (September 1997)

PINT SIZE BOOKS
English

- FINGER FOOD
- PARTY PLANNING
- BUFFETS
- BAKING DELIGHTS
- CHOCOLATE

JEAN PARÉ LIVRES DE CUISINE
French

- 150 DÉLICIEUX CARRÉS
- LES CASSEROLES
- MUFFINS ET PLUS
- LES DÎNERS
- LES BARBECUES
- LES TARTES
- DÉLICES DES FÊTES
- RECETTES LÉGÈRES
- LES SALADES
- LA CUISSON AU MICRO-ONDES
- LES PÂTES
- LES CONSERVES
- LES CASSEROLES LÉGÈRES
- POULET, ETC.
- LA CUISINE POUR LES ENFANTS
- POISSONS ET FRUITS DE MER
- LES PAINS
- LA CUISINE SANS VIANDE
- LA CUISINE POUR DEUX (septembre 1997)

table of Contents

The Jean Paré Story 6
Foreword 7
Glossary 8
Dietary Substitutions 9
Appetizers 10
Beverages 20
Breakfasts 23
Desserts, Cookies, Squares, Etc. 31
Go-Withs 44
Main Courses 49
Pies, Pizzas, Quiches 95
Salads 110
Sandwiches 117
Sauces 130
Soups 133
Vegetables 138
Measurement Tables 151
Index 152
Mail Order Form 157

the Jean Paré story

Jean Paré grew up understanding that the combination of family, friends and home cooking is the essence of a good life. From her mother she learned to appreciate good cooking, while her father praised even her earliest attempts. When she left home she took with her many acquired family recipes, her love of cooking and her intriguing desire to read recipe books like novels!

In 1963, when her four children had all reached school age, Jean volunteered to cater to the 50th anniversary of the Vermilion School of Agriculture, now Lakeland College. Working out of her home, Jean prepared a dinner for over 1000 people which launched a flourishing catering operation that continued for over eighteen years. During that time she was provided with countless opportunities to test new ideas with immediate feedback—resulting in empty plates and contented customers! Whether preparing cocktail sandwiches for a house party or serving a hot meal for 1500 people, Jean Paré earned a reputation for good food, courteous service and reasonable prices.

"Why don't you write a cookbook?" Time and again, as requests for her recipes mounted, Jean was asked that question. Jean's response was to team up with her son, Grant Lovig, in the fall of 1980 to form Company's Coming Publishing Limited. April 14, 1981, marked the debut of "150 DELICIOUS SQUARES", the first Company's Coming cookbook in what soon would become Canada's most popular cookbook series. By 1995, sales had surpassed ten million cookbooks.

Jean Paré's operation has grown from the early days of working out of a spare bedroom in her home to operating a large and fully equipped test kitchen in Vermilion, Alberta, near the home she and her husband Larry built. Full-time staff has grown steadily to include marketing personnel located in major cities across Canada plus selected U.S. markets. Home Office is located in Edmonton, Alberta where distribution, accounting and administration functions are headquartered in the company's own 20,000 square foot facility. Growth continues with the recent addition of the Recipe Factory, a 2700 square foot test kitchen and photography studio located in Edmonton.

Company's Coming cookbooks are now distributed throughout Canada and the United States plus numerous overseas markets, all under the guidance of Jean's daughter, Gail Lovig. The series is published in English and French, plus a Spanish language edition is available in Mexico. Soon the familiar and trusted Company's Coming style of recipes will be available in a variety of formats in addition to the bestselling soft cover series.

Jean Paré's approach to cooking has always called for quick and easy recipes using everyday ingredients. She continues to gain new supporters by adhering to what she calls "the golden rule of cooking": never share a recipe you wouldn't use yourself. It's an approach that works—*ten million times over!*

foreword

This book was written in response to the many inquiries I received from people interested in preparing meatless meals once or twice a week. Most recipes that have been included contain milk products or eggs, but all recipes exclude meat, poultry and fish. Keep in mind that this book should not be considered a promotion or recommendation of any specific diet, nor as a substitute for the advice given by your doctor. Its purpose is simply to provide a wonderful variety of recipes that can be used as alternatives to your usual fare. Included are main courses, appetizers, soups, and even a few high-protein desserts.

An important benefit to meatless cooking is that this style of food preparation often features nutritious ingredients such as vegetables, grains and beans. We sometimes forget to include these food groups in our daily meal planning even though they are cholesterol-free, high in fiber and full of much needed vitamins. Beans, peas and lentils (or legumes as they are sometimes called) are excellent and economical sources of protein. Another benefit is that you will also discover a whole new variety of menu ideas to serve friends and family, be it a complete vegetarian-style dinner or a simple side dish to complement your usual fare.

There are over 150 great recipes to choose from in MEATLESS COOKING. Try a hearty main course dish like Best Roast, page 81 or Zucchini Cutlets, page 87. Jazz up dinner with a tasty side dish such as Corn Chip Salad, page 116, and finish it all off with delicious Tofu Cheesecake, page 38. Add a new dimension to your meal planning when company's coming!

Jean Paré

Each recipe has been analyzed using the most updated version of the Canadian Nutrient File from Health and Welfare Canada which is based upon the United States Department of Agriculture (USDA) Nutrient Data Base.

Margaret Ng, B.Sc. (Hon), M.A., R.D.
Registered Dietitian

GLOSSARY

Arborio Rice: Italian short-grain rice that has a high starch content. It is most often used for Risotto, page 147, but works well in rice puddings and soups containing rice.

Basmati Rice: Long-grain rice that has been aged to reduce moisture content. It should be washed and picked over before cooking. It has a fine texture, a nut-like aroma and flavor, and is used in East Indian and Middle Eastern cooking.

Beans: Seeded pods of various legumes, used in either the fresh or dried state. Dried beans are an excellent source of protein, phosphorus and iron. Fresh beans such as green beans and yellow beans are commonly used in their pods. Lima beans and broad beans are generally eaten shelled. The more popular dried beans are black beans, navy beans, chick peas, kidney beans and pinto beans. To cook 2 cups (500 mL) beans, add 6 cups (1.5 L) water. Another 1 cup (250 mL) boiling water may need to be added later. Simmer pinto, kidney and black beans, covered, about 1 hour. Simmer lima and white (navy, haricot) beans, covered, about 1¾ hours. Garbanzo beans (chick peas) should simmer, covered, about 2¾ hours. Canned beans retain their shape better than cooked dried beans but both will retain excellent flavor. Soaking beans overnight only shortens cooking time by 20 to 30 minutes, however it does reduce sugars that can contribute to digestive gas. If you decide to cook beans from scratch instead of using canned beans, it saves time to cook a large amount. When cool, freeze in 2 cup (500 mL) portions.

Brown Rice: Retains the outer bran coating of the grain, making it higher in fiber than regular white rice. It is nutty in flavor and chewy in texture. It should be stored in an airtight container no longer than 6 months as the bran can go rancid.

Bulgur: Wheat kernels that have been steamed, dried and crushed. Adds a chewy texture to a recipe.

Legumes: Plants that produce seed pods, including beans, peas, lentils, soybeans and peanuts. Legumes are high in protein and also contain fiber, calcium, phosphorous, potassium, fats and most of the B vitamins. Legumes should be washed well and picked over before using.

Lentils: Tiny, lens-shaped legumes. The most common are red, yellow and brown. Good source of protein and potassium, and also contain iron and phosphorus. Lentils cook faster than dried beans, requiring only 30 to 45 minutes.

Nuts: Dry fruits that generally have an edible kernel enclosed in a shell. Nuts provide a good source of calcium, folic acid, magnesium, potassium, vitamin E and fiber. Nuts are also high in mono-unsaturated fats and so have a short shelf life before becoming rancid. To keep nuts fresh, store them in a marked airtight container in the refrigerator up to 4 months, or in the freezer up to 6 months.

Tofu: Made from the curds of soy milk that is then pressed into rectangular shapes. Also known as bean curd. Tofu is high in protein and calcium. Refrigerate covered with water in a covered container. Use within 2 to 3 weeks as it is highly perishable. It can be purchased in soft, medium and firm textures depending on what the recipe calls for or on personal preference.

DIETARY SUBSTITUTIONS

The following list suggests possible ingredient substitutions you can use to help reduce fat or cholesterol, or to replace animal by-products if on a strict vegetarian diet. Please note however that all recipes have been tested using only those ingredients listed in each recipe. Substituting ingredients may vary results.

Cheese: May substitute an equal amount of part-skim or skim cheese to reduce fat. When using part-skim or skim cheese on top of a casserole, sprinkle over top after casserole has been cooked, and return to oven to melt cheese. This cheese forms a dry crust if cooked too long.

Cottage Cheese: May substitute an equal amount of low-fat cottage cheese (less than 1% MF).

Cream Cheese: May substitute an equal amount of low-fat cream cheese (17% MF).

Eggs: May substitute 2 egg whites to replace 1 egg to reduce cholesterol.

Gelatin: May substitute agar-agar to avoid using animal by-products. Gelatin is pure protein derived from beef and veal bones. Agar-agar is made from dried seaweed and can be found in most health food stores. Use 1 tsp. (5 mL) agar-agar for each cup of liquid to be thickened.

Milk: May substitute an equal amount of skim milk to reduce fat.

Sour Cream: May substitute an equal amount of low-fat (7% MF) or non-fat sour cream. Non-fat sour cream is softer and works best on warm or hot foods if mixed in rather than used as a topping. Low-fat (less than 1% MF) or fat-free yogurt may also be substituted for sour cream. Add 2 tbsp. (30 mL) all-purpose flour to 1 cup (250 mL) yogurt to prevent it from going runny during cooking.

Yogurt: May substitute an equal amount of low-fat (less than 1% MF) or fat-free yogurt, or may substitute low-fat (7% MF) or non-fat sour cream.

SAUCED WIENERS

Simmered in a dark sauce, these are really tasty. Very popular.

Black currant jelly preserves	**1 cup**	**250 mL**
Prepared mustard	**2 tsp.**	**10 mL**
Ketchup	**2 tbsp.**	**30 mL**
Soy sauce	**1 tsp.**	**5 mL**
Tofu wieners, cut bite size (or veggie wieners)	**12 oz.**	**340 g**

Measure first 4 ingredients into medium saucepan. Heat and stir until hot.

Add wiener pieces. Bring to a boil. Boil gently until heated through. Transfer to chafing dish. Serve with cocktail picks. Makes about 48 small appetizers.

1 appetizer contains: *28 Calories (118 kJ); trace Fat; 2 g Protein; trace Fiber*

HOT BROCCOLI DIP

The melted cheese makes this a winning combination.

Butter or hard margarine	**2 tbsp.**	**30 mL**
Chopped onion	**1 cup**	**250 mL**
Chopped celery	**1 cup**	**250 mL**
Frozen chopped broccoli	**10 oz.**	**284 g**
Water, to cover		
Condensed cream of mushroom soup	**10 oz.**	**284 mL**
Salt	**1/2 tsp.**	**2 mL**
Garlic powder	**1/4 tsp.**	**1 mL**
Worcestershire sauce	**1 tsp.**	**5 mL**
Cayenne pepper	**1/4 tsp.**	**1 mL**
Grated sharp Cheddar cheese	**1 1/2 cups**	**375 mL**
Assorted crackers		

(continued on next page)

Heat butter in heavy saucepan. Add onion and celery. Sauté until soft.

Cook broccoli in water in separate saucepan. Drain. Add to onion mixture. Stir.

Add next 5 ingredients. Heat, stirring often until mixture starts to simmer.

Add cheese. Stir until it melts.

Turn into chafing dish. Serve with assorted crackers. Makes 3 cups (750 mL).

***2 tbsp. (30 mL) contain:** 56 Calories (234 kJ); 4.3 g Fat; 2 g Protein; 1 g Fiber*

FAR EAST EGGS

Certainly different from the usual devilled eggs. Curry may be increased or decreased.

Large eggs	**6**	**6**
Cold water, to cover		
FILLING		
Cooking oil	**1 tbsp.**	**15 mL**
Finely chopped onion	**½ cup**	**125 mL**
Curry powder	**1 tsp.**	**5 mL**
Ketchup	**2 tbsp.**	**30 mL**
Salt	**¼ tsp.**	**1 mL**
Coarsely chopped raisins	**1 tbsp.**	**15 mL**

Heat eggs in water in saucepan on medium-high until water starts to boil. Boil slowly for 10 minutes. Drain. Cover with cold water 3 or 4 times until eggs are cool. Peel. Cut in half lengthwise. Put yolks into bowl and mash with fork.

Filling: Heat cooking oil in frying pan. Add onion. Sauté until soft and clear.

Stir in curry powder. Cook for 1 minute.

Add ketchup, salt and raisins. Cool. Add to egg yolks. Mix well. Stuff egg whites. Makes 12.

***1 egg contains:** 57 Calories (240 kJ); 3.9 g Fat; 3 g Protein; trace Fiber*

CHILI CON QUESO

Chilee-cahn-KAY-soh is always a winner. A mild chili flavor in a smooth cheese base.

Canned tomatoes, with juice, broken up	**14 oz.**	**398 mL**
Velveeta cheese, cut up (see Note)	**1 lb.**	**454 g**
Canned diced green chilies	**4 oz.**	**114 mL**
Minced onion	**1 tbsp.**	**15 mL**

Tortilla chips, potato chips, corn chips

Combine first 4 ingredients in top of double boiler. Heat, stirring often, over simmering water. Heat slowly. If heated too fast or too hot, cheese may go stringy.

Serve warm with your choice of an assortment of chips. Makes 3¾ cups (850 mL).

Note: If Velveeta cheese is not available, use another mild, soft, process cheese.

2 tbsp. (30 mL) contain: *52 Calories (217 kJ); 3.6 g Fat; 3 g Protein; trace Fiber*

HUMMUS

Light in color, tasty and nutty in flavor. HOOM-uhs has a bit of a lemony tang.

Chick peas (garbanzo beans), drained and liquid reserved	**19 oz.**	**540 mL**
Lemon juice, fresh or bottled	**¼ cup**	**60 mL**
Tahini (sesame spread), page 49	**⅓ cup**	**75 mL**
Garlic powder	**½ tsp.**	**2 mL**
Onion powder	**¼ tsp.**	**1 mL**
Salt	**½ tsp.**	**2 mL**
Pepper	**⅛ tsp.**	**0.5 mL**
Reserved chick pea liquid	**6 tbsp.**	**100 mL**

Parsley, for garnish
Crackers, bread cubes, raw vegetables or tortilla chips

(continued on next page)

Pour chick peas and lemon juice into blender. Process until smooth.

Add tahini, garlic powder, onion powder, salt and pepper. Process to mix. Add reserved liquid as needed to thin so it is like soft whipped cream. Can be served in bowl or on bed of lettuce.

Garnish with parsley. Serve with crackers, bread, raw vegetables or tortilla chips. Makes 2½ cups (575 mL).

***2 tbsp. (30 mL) contain:** 55 Calories (229 kJ); 2.4 g Fat; 2 g Protein; 1 g Fiber*

BAKED CHEESE BALLS

There is a hidden treasure in each of these. Pastry is wrapped around a green olive before baking.

Process cheese spread containing aged Cheddar (such as Ingersoll), room temperature	**1 cup**	**250 mL**
All-purpose flour	**1½ cups**	**375 mL**
Butter or hard margarine, softened	**½ cup**	**125 mL**
Cayenne pepper	**½ tsp.**	**2 mL**
Whole pimiento-stuffed green olives	**10-40**	**10-40**

Mix cheese, flour, butter and cayenne well until blended. Shape into 2 long rolls, equal in length. Mark off, then cut each roll into 20 pieces. Roll into balls. Flatten each ball between your fingers.

Shape around whole olive. Some can be shaped into balls without olives, if desired. Arrange on ungreased baking sheet. Bake in 400°F (205°C) oven for about 10 minutes. You can also freeze these unbaked on a baking sheet, then store in plastic container in freezer to bake another time. Makes 40 tiny cheese balls.

***1 ball contains:** 63 Calories (263 kJ); 4.3 g Fat; 2 g Protein; trace Fiber*

Paré Pointer

A man wears trousers; a dog pants.

STUFFED MUSHROOMS

Carrots add color. Always a popular choice for an appetizer.

Medium fresh mushrooms	**18**	**18**
Butter or hard margarine	**2 tbsp.**	**30 mL**
Chopped mushroom stems		
Finely chopped onion	**1/4 cup**	**60 mL**
Grated carrot	**1/4 cup**	**60 mL**
Salt	**1/2 tsp.**	**2 mL**
Pepper	**1/8 tsp.**	**0.5 mL**
Ground almonds	**1/4 cup**	**60 mL**
Grated Parmesan cheese, sprinkle		

Gently twist stems from mushrooms. Chop stems.

Melt butter in frying pan. Add next 5 ingredients. Sauté until onion is soft. Remove from heat.

Stir in almonds. Stuff mushroom caps. Arrange on ungreased baking sheet. Sprinkle with Parmesan cheese. Bake in 400°F (205°C) oven for 10 to 12 minutes. Makes 18 appetizers.

1 appetizer contains: *26 Calories (108 kJ); 2.1 g Fat; 1 g Protein; trace Fiber*

GUACAMOLE

Mildly zesty, this dip is a popular one.

Ripe avocados, peeled and mashed	**2**	**2**
Lemon juice, fresh or bottled	**2 tbsp.**	**30 mL**
Medium tofu, drained and mashed	**1 cup**	**250 mL**
Green onions, finely chopped	**2**	**2**
Chili powder	**1 tsp.**	**5 mL**
Salt	**1/2 tsp.**	**2 mL**
Pepper	**1/8 tsp.**	**0.5 mL**
Garlic powder	**1/4 tsp.**	**1 mL**
Cayenne pepper	**1/8 tsp.**	**0.5 mL**
Medium tomatoes, seeded and diced	**2**	**2**
Raw vegetables, corn chips and tortilla chips		

(continued on next page)

Mix first 9 ingredients well in medium bowl.

Fold in diced tomato. Serve soon, as mixture tends to darken because of the avocado.

Serve with raw vegetables, corn chips and tortilla chips. Makes 2½ cups (575 mL).

2 tbsp. (30 mL) contain: *53 Calories (223 kJ); 4.1 g Fat; 3 g Protein; 1 g Fiber*

BLACK BEAN DIP

A darkish dip with cheese sprinkled over top. Cider vinegar gives it a good tang.

Canned black beans, drained	**19 oz.**	**540 mL**
Cider vinegar	**2 tsp.**	**10 mL**
Salt	**½ tsp.**	**2 mL**
Pepper	**⅛ tsp.**	**0.5 mL**
Garlic powder	**¼ tsp.**	**1 mL**
Onion powder	**¼ tsp.**	**1 mL**
Hot pepper sauce (optional)	**¼-½ tsp.**	**1-2 mL**
TOPPING		
Grated medium Cheddar cheese	**¼ cup**	**60 mL**
Ground walnuts	**1 tbsp.**	**15 mL**
Tortilla chips, corn chips or raw vegetables		

Mash beans well with fork on plate. Turn into bowl.

Add next 6 ingredients. Stir. Transfer to serving dish.

Topping: Sprinkle cheese and walnuts over top. Chill until needed.

Serve with tortilla chips, corn chips or raw vegetables. Makes 1⅓ cups (300 mL).

2 tbsp. (30 mL) contain: *71 Calories (298 kJ); 1.5 g Fat; 5 g Protein; 2 g Fiber*

CHEESE SPREAD

This spread is speckled throughout. Best served at room temperature with crackers, raw vegetables or fruit.

Process cheese spread, room temperature	**1 cup**	**250 mL**
Cream cheese, softened	**12 oz.**	**375 g**
Blue cheese, crumbled, softened	**4 oz.**	**125 g**
Butter or hard margarine, softened	**¼ cup**	**60 mL**
Finely grated onion	**1 tbsp.**	**15 mL**
Worcestershire sauce	**1 tsp.**	**5 mL**
Garlic powder	**¼ tsp.**	**1 mL**
Ground pecans	**½ cup**	**125 mL**
Chopped fresh parsley (or 2 tsp., 10 mL, flakes)	**¼ cup**	**60 mL**
Ground pecans	**½ cup**	**125 mL**
Chopped fresh parsley (or 2 tsp., 10 mL, flakes)	**¼ cup**	**60 mL**

Place first 9 ingredients into bowl. Beat well. Pack into shallow bowl.

Sprinkle with pecans and parsley. Makes 3½ cups (800 mL).

1 tbsp. (15 mL) contains: *68 Calories (286 kJ); 6.4 g Fat; 2 g Protein; trace Fiber*

1. Fruit Shake, page 21
2. Orange Yogurt Drink, page 21
3. Chocolate Yogurt Drink, page 21
4. Cheese Strata, page 24
5. Spinach Roulade, page 148

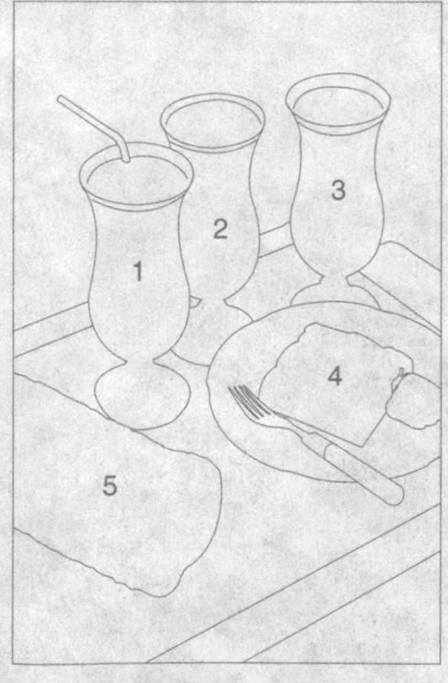

1. Tray, Glasses And Dinnerware Courtesy Of: The Bay
2. Flatware Courtesy Of: IKEA
3. Placemat Courtesy Of: La Cache

CHEESE NUGGETS

Little seed-capped mounds. Curry flavor is excellent.

Butter or hard margarine, softened	**½ cup**	**125 mL**
All-purpose flour (or whole wheat)	**1 cup**	**250 mL**
Grated sharp Cheddar cheese	**1 cup**	**250 mL**
Curry powder	**1 tsp.**	**5 mL**
Egg yolk (large)	**1**	**1**
Egg white (large), fork-beaten	**1**	**1**
Toasted sesame seeds	**2 tbsp.**	**30 mL**

Mix butter and flour well. Add cheese and curry powder. Mix. Stir in egg yolk. Shape into small balls, using about 2 tsp. (10 mL) dough for each.

Dip tops of balls in egg white in small bowl. Shake off excess. Dip in sesame seeds. Arrange on ungreased baking sheet. Bake in 375°F (190°C) oven for about 15 minutes. Makes about 30 nuggets.

***1 nugget contains:** 67 Calories (281 kJ); 5.1 g Fat; 2 g Protein; trace Fiber*

BAKED CHEESE

A round of nutty coated cheese that is just yummy.

Brie or Camembert cheese round	**1 × 4½ oz.**	**1 × 125 g**
Butter or hard margarine, softened	**2 tbsp.**	**30 mL**
Brown sugar, packed	**2 tbsp.**	**30 mL**
Sliced hazelnuts	**¼ cup**	**60 mL**
Toast squares, assorted crackers or dark bread squares		

Place cheese in ungreased pie plate.

Cream butter and sugar in bowl. Spread over top and sides of cheese.

Sprinkle top with nuts. Press lightly into cheese. Bake, uncovered, in 350°F (175°C) oven for 15 to 20 minutes to heat through. Makes 1 cheese round.

Serve with toast, crackers or bread.

***1 tbsp. (15 mL) contains:** 157 Calories (656 kJ); 13 g Fat; 6 g Protein; trace Fiber*

PINEAPPLE YOGURT DRINK

Cream-colored with a pineapple flavor.

Plain yogurt	**1 cup**	**250 mL**
Crushed pineapple, with juice	**½ × 14 oz.**	**½ × 398 mL**
Granulated sugar	**2 tsp.**	**10 mL**

Combine all 3 ingredients in blender. Process until smooth. Makes 1¾ cups (425 mL), enough for 2 small servings.

1 serving contains: *161 Calories (673 kJ); 2.1 g Fat; 7 g Protein; 1 g Fiber*

STRAWBERRY SHAKE

A great shake using yogurt instead of ice cream.

Plain yogurt	**1 cup**	**250 mL**
Chopped frozen whole strawberries	**1 cup**	**250 mL**
Brown sugar, packed	**2 tbsp.**	**30 mL**

Put yogurt, strawberries and brown sugar into blender. Process until smooth. Makes 1¾ cups (425 mL), enough for 2 small servings.

1 serving contains: *161 Calories (674 kJ); 2.1 g Fat; 7 g Protein; 1 g Fiber*

TOFU SHAKE

So thick, with a hint of cinnamon.

Firm tofu, cut up	**8 oz.**	**250 g**
Crushed pineapple, with juice	**14 oz.**	**398 mL**
Brown sugar, packed	**2 tbsp.**	**30 mL**
Ground cinnamon	**¼ tsp.**	**1 mL**

Measure all 4 ingredients into blender. Process until smooth. Makes 2⅔ cups (600 mL), enough for 2 large servings.

1 serving contains: *360 Calories (1507 kJ); 11.1 g Fat; 21 g Protein; 2 g Fiber*

FRUIT SHAKE

A combination of some banana split ingredients. Excellent.

Plain yogurt	**1 cup**	**250 mL**
Chopped frozen whole strawberries	**1 cup**	**250 mL**
Banana, cut up	**1**	**1**
Brown sugar, packed	**2 tbsp.**	**30 mL**
Chopped walnuts	**¼ cup**	**60 mL**

Measure all 5 ingredients into blender. Process until smooth. Makes 2 cups (500 mL), enough for 2 servings.

1 serving contains: *321 Calories (1342 kJ); 12.7 g Fat; 10 g Protein; 3 g Fiber*

Pictured on page 17.

ORANGE YOGURT DRINK

A refreshing drink that isn't sweet.

Plain yogurt	**1 cup**	**250 mL**
Milk	**1 cup**	**250 mL**
Frozen concentrated orange juice	**¼ cup**	**60 mL**

Combine yogurt, milk and concentrated orange juice in blender. Process until smooth. Makes 3 cups (750 mL), enough for 3 servings.

1 serving contains: *137 Calories (574 kJ); 3 g Fat; 8 g Protein; trace Fiber*

Pictured on page 17.

CHOCOLATE YOGURT DRINK

Medium thick with a mellow chocolate flavor.

Plain yogurt	**1 cup**	**250 mL**
Milk	**½ cup**	**125 mL**
Brown sugar	**2 tsp.**	**10 mL**
Chocolate drink powder	**2 tbsp.**	**30 mL**

Measure all 4 ingredients into blender. Process until smooth. Makes 1¾ cups (425 mL), enough for 2 small servings.

1 serving contains: *169 Calories (705 kJ); 3.6 g Fat; 9 g Protein; trace Fiber*

Pictured on page 17.

CRANBERRY PUNCH

A pretty rosy blush color gives this an appealing look. Nice flavor.

Cranberry cocktail	**2 cups**	**500 mL**
Whole cloves	**6**	**6**
Cranberry cocktail	**3 cups**	**750 mL**
Lemon juice, fresh or bottled	**1/4 cup**	**60 mL**
Apple juice	**2 cups**	**500 mL**
Orange flavoring	**1/2 tsp.**	**2 mL**
Ginger ale	**5 cups**	**1.25 L**
Ice cubes		
Orange slices, paper thin	**4-8**	**4-8**

Bring first amount of cranberry cocktail and cloves to a boil. Boil for 1 minute. Cool by placing saucepan in cold water. Discard cloves. Pour into punch bowl.

Add next 4 ingredients. Chill until ready to serve.

Add ginger ale. Stir gently. Carefully add ice cubes.

Float orange slices on top. Makes 12 cups (3 L), enough for 12 servings.

1 serving contains: *123 Calories (516 kJ); trace Fat; trace Protein; trace Fiber*

GRAPEFRUIT PUNCH

This is a good refreshing drink. Not too sweet but just right.

Grapefruit juice (pink or white), chilled	**4 1/2 cups**	**1 L**
Apple juice	**3 cups**	**750 mL**
Granulated sugar	**1 cup**	**250 mL**
Ginger ale	**4 1/2 cups**	**1 L**
Ice cubes		

Stir grapefruit juice, apple juice and sugar together in bowl until sugar dissolves. Chill until ready to use. Pour into punch bowl.

Add ginger ale. Stir gently. Carefully add ice cubes. Makes about 12 cups (3 L), enough for 12 servings.

1 serving contains: *161 Calories (673 kJ); trace Fat; trace Protein; trace Fiber*

PEACHES AND CREAM

Creamy yellow, this frothy drink has a peach flavor.

Canned sliced peaches, with juice	**14 oz.**	**398 mL**
Plain yogurt	**1 cup**	**250 mL**
Brown sugar, packed	**2 tbsp.**	**30 mL**

Place peaches along with juice, yogurt and brown sugar in blender. Process until smooth. Makes 2⅔ cups (650 mL), enough for 2 large servings.

1 serving contains: *225 Calories (943 kJ); 2.1 g Fat; 8 g Protein; 2 g Fiber*

FRUITY YOGURT DRINK

Creamy beige color. All flavors can be tasted.

Plain yogurt	**1 cup**	**250 mL**
Banana, cut up	**1**	**1**
Pineapple juice	**1 cup**	**250 mL**

Combine yogurt, banana and pineapple juice in blender. Process until smooth. Makes 2½ cups (625 mL), enough for 2 large servings.

1 serving contains: *184 Calories (771 kJ); trace Fat; 2 g Protein; 2 g Fiber*

PANCAKE SYRUP

So simple to make your own. Store in refrigerator. May be reheated if sugar crystals form.

Brown sugar, packed	**2¼ cups**	**550 mL**
Granulated sugar	**¾ cup**	**175 mL**
Water	**1½ cups**	**375 mL**
Corn syrup	**2 tbsp.**	**30 mL**
Maple flavoring	**1 tsp.**	**5 mL**

Measure all 5 ingredients into medium saucepan. Heat and bring to a boil, stirring often. Boil slowly for about 10 minutes. Makes 2⅔ cups (650 mL).

2 tbsp. (30 mL) contain: *122 Calories (510 kJ); 0 g Fat; 0 g Protein; trace Fiber*

CHEESE STRATA

An orange-yellow puff dish. Enjoy this hot cheese sandwich.

White bread slices, buttered, crusts removed	**4**	**4**
Grated medium or sharp Cheddar cheese	**1 cup**	**250 mL**
White bread slices, buttered, crusts removed	**4**	**4**
Grated medium or sharp Cheddar cheese	**1 cup**	**250 mL**
Large eggs	**3**	**3**
Milk	**2 cups**	**500 mL**
Dry mustard powder	**1/2 tsp.**	**2 mL**
Salt	**1/2 tsp.**	**2 mL**

Line bottom of ungreased 8 × 8 inch (20 × 20 cm) pan with first slices of bread, buttered side down. Sprinkle with first amount of cheese. Cover cheese with second slices of bread, buttered side up. Sprinkle with second amount of cheese.

Beat eggs in bowl. Add milk, mustard and salt. Beat to mix. Pour over cheese and bread. Cover. Store overnight in refrigerator. Remove cover. Bake in 350°F (175°C) oven for about 45 minutes. For a double recipe, bake in ungreased 9 × 13 inch (22 × 33 cm) pan in oven for about 1 hour. Single recipe makes 6 servings.

1 serving contains: *329 Calories (1375 kJ); 21 g Fat; 18 g Protein; trace Fiber*

Pictured on page 17.

SPINACH NESTS

The logical place to find eggs—in a nest. Increase recipe as needed.

Frozen chopped spinach	**2 × 10 oz.**	**2 × 300 g**
Boiling water, to cover		
Salt	**1/2 tsp.**	**2 mL**
Pepper	**1/8 tsp.**	**0.5 mL**
Ground nutmeg	**1/8 tsp.**	**0.5 mL**
Large eggs	**4**	**4**
Simmering water, to cover		

(continued on next page)

Cook spinach in boiling water for about 6 minutes until done. Drain.

Add salt, pepper and nutmeg. Stir to mix. Keep warm while preparing eggs.

Poach eggs in simmering water. Make 4 nests of spinach on warmed plates. Using a slotted spoon, place an egg in each nest. Makes 4 nests.

1 nest contains: *117 Calories (490 kJ); 5.4 g Fat; 11 g Protein; 5 g Fiber*

BAKED OMELET

Exc.

Here are bacon and eggs in one dish.

Plain croutons (or cut up toast)	**2 cups**	**500 mL**
Grated medium Cheddar cheese	**1 cup**	**250 mL**
Veggie back bacon slices, cut into small bite size pieces	**6**	**6**
Large eggs	**6**	**6**
Dry mustard powder	**½ tsp.**	**2 mL**
Salt	**½ tsp.**	**2 mL**
Pepper	**⅛ tsp.**	**0.5 mL**
Onion powder	**⅛ tsp.**	**0.5 mL**
Milk	**2 cups**	**500 mL**

Spread croutons in greased 8 × 8 inch (20 × 20 cm) pan. Sprinkle cheese over top followed by veggie bacon.

Beat eggs in bowl. Add mustard powder, salt, pepper and onion powder. Beat to mix.

Add milk. Mix. Pour over bacon. Bake, uncovered, in 325°F (160°C) oven for about 45 minutes until set. Serves 6.

1 serving contains: *277 Calories (1154 kJ); 14 g Fat; 21 g Protein; trace Fiber*

WHEAT PANCAKES

These are both healthy and tender.

Whole wheat flour	**1½ cups**	**375 mL**
All-purpose flour	**1 cup**	**250 mL**
Granulated sugar	**1 tbsp.**	**15 mL**
Baking powder	**1 tbsp.**	**15 mL**
Baking soda	**½ tsp.**	**2 mL**
Salt	**½ tsp.**	**2 mL**
Large egg, fork-beaten	**1**	**1**
Cooking oil	**1½ tbsp.**	**25 mL**
Buttermilk, fresh or reconstituted from powder	**2 cups**	**500 mL**

Stir first 6 ingredients together in bowl.

Add remaining ingredients. Stir just to moisten. Add a bit more milk if needed for a thinner pancake. Drop about ¼ cup (60 mL) batter onto hot greased frying pan. When bubbles appear and edges look dry, turn to cook other side. Pan won't need to be greased between batches. Serve with Pancake Syrup, page 23. Makes 14 pancakes.

1 pancake contains: *120 Calories (502 kJ); 2.7 g Fat; 5 g Protein; 2 g Fiber*

APPLE RAISIN PANCAKES

Pancakes at their best. Choose to have them fruity, or fruity and nutty.

All-purpose flour	**¾ cup**	**175 mL**
Whole wheat flour	**¾ cup**	**175 mL**
Brown sugar, packed	**2 tbsp.**	**30 mL**
Baking powder	**2 tsp.**	**10 mL**
Baking soda	**½ tsp.**	**2 mL**
Salt	**¼ tsp.**	**1 mL**
Large egg	**1**	**1**
Cooking oil	**2 tbsp.**	**30 mL**
Unsweetened applesauce	**14 oz.**	**398 mL**
Ground cinnamon	**½ tsp.**	**2 mL**
Raisins	**½ cup**	**125 mL**
Milk, approximately (as needed to thin)	**¼ cup**	**60 mL**

(continued on next page)

Measure first 6 ingredients into bowl. Stir.

Add remaining ingredients. Mix until moistened. Drop about 1/4 cup (60 mL) at a time onto hot greased frying pan. When bubbles appear and edges look dry, turn to cook other side. Serve with butter and Pancake Syrup, page 23. Makes 12 pancakes.

1 pancake contains: *134 Calories (559 kJ); 3.1 g Fat; 3 g Protein; 2 g Fiber*

NUTTY FRUIT PANCAKES: Add 1/4 cup (60 mL) sunflower seeds.

FRUITIER PANCAKES: Add 1 banana, diced.

YOGURT BRAN PANCAKES

Yogurt and bran cereal combine to make these extra good. A breakfast or lunch treat.

Large egg	**1**	**1**
All-bran cereal (100%)	**1 cup**	**250 mL**
Plain yogurt	**1 cup**	**250 mL**
Milk	**3/4 cup**	**175 mL**
Cooking oil	**1 tbsp.**	**15 mL**
All-purpose flour	**1 cup**	**250 mL**
Brown sugar, packed	**3 tbsp.**	**50 mL**
Baking powder	**1 tbsp.**	**15 mL**
Salt	**1/2 tsp.**	**2 mL**

Beat egg with spoon in bowl. Mix in bran, yogurt, milk and cooking oil.

Add remaining ingredients. Stir just to moisten. Drop about 1/4 cup (60 mL) onto hot greased frying pan. When edges appear dry and bubbles have formed on top, turn to cook other side. Pan won't need to be greased between batches. Serve with maple syrup or Pancake Syrup, page 23. Makes about 13 pancakes.

1 pancake contains: *99 Calories (413 kJ); 2.3 g Fat; 4 g Protein; 2 g Fiber*

EGGS ON TOAST

A surprise is the cheese spread on the toast before the egg is added. A red flecked sauce covers all.

PIMIENTO SAUCE		
Butter or hard margarine	**2 tbsp.**	**30 mL**
All-purpose flour	**2 tbsp.**	**30 mL**
Salt	**$\frac{1}{2}$ tsp.**	**2 mL**
Pepper	**$\frac{1}{16}$ tsp.**	**0.5 mL**
Chopped pimiento	**1 tbsp.**	**15 mL**
Milk	**1 cup**	**250 mL**
Brown bread slices, toasted (or 2 English muffins or hamburger buns, split and toasted)	**4**	**4**
Softened sharp cheese (such as Imperial or Ingersoll spread)	**4 tbsp.**	**60 mL**
Poached eggs	**4**	**4**

Pimiento Sauce: Melt butter in saucepan. Mix in flour, salt and pepper. Stir in pimiento and milk until mixture boils and thickens.

Spread each slice of toast with 1 tbsp. (15 mL) of cheese.

Place an egg on each toast slice. Spoon sauce over top. Serves 4.

1 serving contains: *280 Calories (1139 kJ); 16.2 g Fat; 14 g Protein; 3 g Fiber*

CHEESE-SAUCED EGGS

Pass a dish of hard-boiled eggs, halved, covered with a cheesy sauce. Now pass the toast.

Butter or hard margarine	**$1\frac{1}{2}$ tbsp.**	**25 mL**
All-purpose flour	**$1\frac{1}{2}$ tbsp.**	**25 mL**
Salt	**$\frac{1}{2}$ tsp.**	**2 mL**
Pepper	**$\frac{1}{8}$ tsp.**	**0.5 mL**
Milk	**1 cup**	**250 mL**
Grated medium or sharp Cheddar cheese	**1 cup**	**250 mL**
Hard-boiled eggs, warm and halved (see Note)	**6**	**6**
Paprika, sprinkle		

(continued on next page)

Melt butter in saucepan. Mix in flour, salt and pepper. Stir in milk until mixture boils and thickens.

Add cheese. Stir to melt.

Arrange egg halves in shallow serving bowl. Pour cheese sauce over top. Sprinkle with paprika. Makes 6 servings of 2 halves each.

Note: To keep eggs warm, have them cooking while making sauce. Cool enough to remove shells. Place in hot water until ready to serve.

1 serving contains: *216 Calories (903 kJ); 16 g Fat; 13 g Protein; trace Fiber*

COTTAGE CHEESE PANCAKES

Whether you use tofu in these or not, the flavor is delicious.

Large eggs	**2**	**2**
Creamed cottage cheese	**1 cup**	**250 mL**
Peeled, grated cooking apple, packed (McIntosh is good)	**1¼ cups**	**300 mL**
Brown sugar, packed	**2 tbsp.**	**30 mL**
Lemon juice, fresh or bottled	**1 tsp.**	**5 mL**
All-purpose flour	**1 cup**	**250 mL**
Baking powder	**2 tsp.**	**10 mL**
Baking soda	**½ tsp.**	**2 mL**
Salt	**½ tsp.**	**2 mL**
Ground cinnamon	**½ tsp.**	**2 mL**
Milk, approximately (as needed to thin)	**¼ cup**	**60 mL**

Beat eggs in bowl with spoon. Mix in cottage cheese, apple, brown sugar and lemon juice.

Stir in remaining ingredients to moisten. Drop by ¼ cup (60 mL) onto hot greased frying pan. Turn to brown other side when surface is bubbly and edges look dry. Serve with Pancake Syrup, page 23. Makes 12 pancakes.

1 pancake contains: *94 Calories (395 kJ); 2.1 g Fat; 5 g Protein; 1 g Fiber*

TOFU PANCAKES: Omit cottage cheese. Use same amount of soft tofu, mashed, instead. Works well.

BRUNCH CAKE

Have your cereal and fruit in a coffee cake.

Bran flakes cereal	**1 cup**	**250 mL**
Prepared orange juice	**1 cup**	**250 mL**
Cooking oil	**1/4 cup**	**60 mL**
Large egg	**1**	**1**
Small bananas, thinly sliced	**2**	**2**
All-purpose flour	**1 1/2 cups**	**375 mL**
Granulated sugar	**3/4 cup**	**175 mL**
Raisins	**1/2 cup**	**125 mL**
Baking soda	**1 tsp.**	**5 mL**
Ground cinnamon	**1 tsp.**	**5 mL**
Salt	**1/2 tsp.**	**2 mL**
STREUSEL TOPPING		
Brown sugar, packed	**3/4 cup**	**175 mL**
Chopped walnuts or pecans	**3/4 cup**	**175 mL**
All-purpose flour	**6 tbsp.**	**100 mL**
Ground cinnamon	**3/4 tsp.**	**4 mL**
Butter or hard margarine, softened	**6 tbsp.**	**100 mL**

Stir bran flakes and orange juice together in medium bowl. Let stand for 5 minutes until soft.

Add cooking oil, egg and banana. Stir.

Stir in remaining 6 ingredients. Pour into greased 9 × 13 inch (22 × 33 cm) pan. Bake in 350°F (175°C) oven for about 30 minutes until cake springs back when lightly touched.

Streusel Topping: Combine brown sugar, walnuts, flour and cinnamon in bowl. Stir. Mix in butter until crumbly. Spread over hot cake. Heat broiler. Broil about 5 inches (12 cm) from heat about 1 minute until bubbly. Serve warm or at room temperature. Serves 15.

1 serving contains: *315 Calories (1320 kJ); 13.3 g Fat; 4 g Protein; 2 g Fiber*

Sign on a lunchroom window: Quiche me, I'm French!

ORANGE DATE LOAF

A large loaf with a wonderfully bold orange flavor.

Large eggs	**2**	**2**
Butter or hard margarine, softened	**½ cup**	**125 mL**
Brown sugar, packed	**1 cup**	**250 mL**
Prepared orange juice	**½ cup**	**125 mL**
Whole orange, with peel, cut up and seeded	**1**	**1**
Chopped dates	**1 cup**	**250 mL**
All-purpose flour	**2½ cups**	**625 mL**
Baking powder	**1 tsp.**	**5 mL**
Baking soda	**1 tsp.**	**5 mL**
Salt	**½ tsp.**	**2 mL**

Beat eggs, butter, brown sugar and orange juice in bowl until blended.

Grind orange and dates in food chopper. Add to egg mixture and stir.

Stir last 4 ingredients together in separate bowl. Add. Stir just to moisten. Turn into greased 9 × 5 × 3 inch (22 × 12 × 7 cm) loaf pan. Bake in 350°F (175°C) oven for 65 to 70 minutes until an inserted wooden pick comes out clean. Makes 1 loaf, 16 slices.

***1 slice contains:** 227 Calories (949 kJ); 7 g Fat; 3 g Protein; 2 g Fiber*

The skin specialist told the teenager he wouldn't make rash promises.

PINEAPPLE CHEESE DESSERT

There is a layer of pineapple hidden under the cheesecake topping. Excellent choice.

CRUST		
Butter or hard margarine	1/3 cup	75 mL
Graham cracker crumbs	1 1/4 cups	300 mL
Brown sugar, packed	2 tbsp.	30 mL
SECOND LAYER		
Granulated sugar	1/2 cup	125 mL
Cornstarch	2 tbsp.	30 mL
Canned crushed pineapple, with juice	14 oz.	398 mL
THIRD LAYER		
Light cream cheese, softened	12 oz.	375 g
Granulated sugar	3/4 cup	175 mL
Salt	3/4 tsp.	4 mL
Large eggs	4	4
Milk	1 cup	250 mL
Vanilla	1/2 tsp.	2 mL
TOPPING		
Chopped pecans	1/4 cup	60 mL

Crust: Melt butter in saucepan. Stir in graham crumbs and brown sugar. Press in bottom of ungreased 9 × 9 inch (22 × 22 cm) pan.

Second Layer: Stir granulated sugar and cornstarch in saucepan. Add pineapple with juice. Heat and stir until mixture boils and thickens. Cool. Spread over prepared crust.

Third Layer: Beat cream cheese, granulated sugar and salt until soft. Beat in eggs, 1 at a time. Add milk and vanilla. Beat. Pour over pineapple layer.

Topping: Sprinkle with pecans. Bake in 400°F (205°C) oven for 10 minutes. Reduce heat to 325°F (160°C). Continue to bake for 50 minutes more. A knife inserted near center should come out clean. After removing from oven, immediately run sharp knife around top edge to allow sides to settle evenly. Cool. Cuts into 12 pieces.

1 piece contains: *331 Calories (1385 kJ); 15.6 g Fat; 8 g Protein; 1 g Fiber*

ZUCCHINI FRUIT BARS

A cake-like panful glazed and sprinkled with nuts. Feeds a crowd.

Butter or hard margarine, softened	**3/4 cup**	**175 mL**
Brown sugar, packed	**1/2 cup**	**125 mL**
Granulated sugar	**1/2 cup**	**125 mL**
Large eggs	**2**	**2**
Vanilla	**1 tsp.**	**5 mL**
All-purpose flour	**1 3/4 cups**	**425 mL**
Baking powder	**1 1/2 tsp.**	**7 mL**
Salt	**1/4 tsp.**	**1 mL**
Medium coconut	**3/4 cup**	**175 mL**
Raisins	**3/4 cup**	**175 mL**
Chopped dates (or additional raisins)	**3/4 cup**	**175 mL**
Grated zucchini, with peel	**2 1/2 cups**	**625 mL**
SPICY NUT ICING		
Butter or hard margarine	**1 tbsp.**	**15 mL**
Milk	**2 tbsp.**	**30 mL**
Vanilla	**1 tsp.**	**5 mL**
Icing (confectioner's) sugar	**1 cup**	**250 mL**
Ground cinnamon	**1/2 tsp.**	**2 mL**
Chopped walnuts	**3/4 cup**	**175 mL**

Cream butter and both sugars in mixing bowl. Beat in eggs, 1 at a time. Add vanilla. Mix.

Add flour, baking powder and salt. Mix.

Add coconut, raisins, dates and zucchini. Stir well. Spread in greased 10 × 15 inch (25 × 38 cm) jelly roll pan. Bake in 350°F (175°C) oven for 30 to 35 minutes until an inserted wooden pick comes out clean.

Spicy Nut Icing: Measure first 5 ingredients into saucepan. Heat and stir until butter melts and mixture is thin and smooth. Spread over warm bars.

Sprinkle with walnuts. Cuts into 66 squares.

1 square contains: *83 Calories (347 kJ); 4.1 g Fat; 1 g Protein; 1 g Fiber*

FRUIT AND NUT DESSERT

So easy to prepare and scrumptious to eat.

Canned cherry pie filling	**19 oz.**	**540 mL**
Canned crushed pineapple, with juice	**19 oz.**	**540 mL**
Almond flavoring	**1/2 tsp.**	**2 mL**
Liquid honey	**3 tbsp.**	**50 mL**
Butter or hard margarine	**1/4 cup**	**60 mL**
Water	**1/2 cup**	**125 mL**
Yellow cake mix, 2 layer size	**1**	**1**
Ground pecans	**1 cup**	**250 mL**
Whole pecans, for garnish		

Mix first 4 ingredients in bowl. Spread in greased 9 × 13 inch (22 × 33 cm) pan.

Melt butter in large saucepan. Add water. Stir in cake mix until evenly moist.

Add ground pecans to cake mixture. Dab evenly over cherry mixture. Spread as best you can. Garnish with whole pecans. Bake in 350°F (175°C) oven for about 45 minutes. Serve warm. Cuts into 15 pieces.

1 piece contains: *305 Calories (1275 kJ); 12.3 g Fat; 2 g Protein; 1 g Fiber*

Pictured on page 35.

1. Peas Deluxe, page 141
2. Fruit And Nut Dessert, page 34
3. Sandwiched Nut Loaf, page 79
4. Red Onion Salsa, page 46
5. Best Roast, page 81

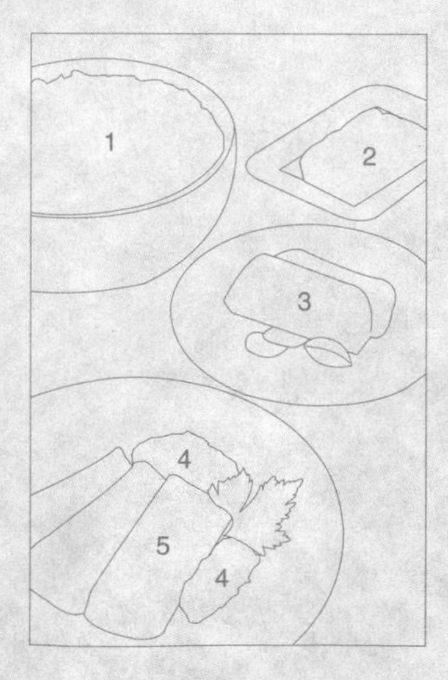

Throw And Dinnerware Courtesy Of:
Chintz & Company

Flowers Courtesy Of:
The Bay

RAISIN COOKIES

Spicy, fruity and nutty. Makes a large batch but they will go fast.

Water	**1 cup**	**250 mL**
Raisins	**2 cups**	**500 mL**
Butter or hard margarine, softened	**1 cup**	**250 mL**
Granulated sugar	**1 cup**	**250 mL**
Brown sugar, packed	**1 cup**	**250 mL**
Large eggs	**3**	**3**
Vanilla	**1 tsp.**	**5 mL**
All-purpose flour	**3¾ cups**	**925 mL**
Baking powder	**1 tsp.**	**5 mL**
Baking soda	**1 tsp.**	**5 mL**
Salt	**1 tsp.**	**5 mL**
Ground cinnamon	**1½ tsp.**	**7 mL**
Ground nutmeg	**¼ tsp.**	**1 mL**
Ground allspice	**¼ tsp.**	**1 mL**
Chopped walnuts or pecans (optional)	**1 cup**	**250 mL**

Cook water and raisins in saucepan for 5 minutes. Cool.

Cream butter and both sugars in large bowl. Beat in eggs, 1 at a time. Add vanilla and raisin-water mixture. Mix.

Add next 8 ingredients. Mix. Drop by rounded tablespoonfuls onto greased cookie sheet. Bake in 350°F (175°C) oven for 10 to 12 minutes until well browned. Makes about 5 dozen cookies.

1 cookie contains: *106 Calories (444 kJ); 3.6 g Fat; 1 g Protein; trace Fiber*

Some people keep their watches on chains so they don't lose time.

TOFU CHEESECAKE

A wonderful cheesecake texture. Strawberry sauce finishes off this dessert.

GRAHAM CRACKER CRUST		
Butter or hard margarine	**3 tbsp.**	**50 mL**
Graham cracker crumbs	**3/4 cup**	**175 mL**
Brown sugar	**2 tsp.**	**10 mL**
FILLING		
Large eggs	**3**	**3**
Medium firm tofu, cut up	**1 lb.**	**454 g**
Cream cheese, cut up	**8 oz.**	**250 g**
All-purpose flour	**1/4 cup**	**60 mL**
Granulated sugar	**3/4 cup**	**175 mL**
Lemon juice, fresh or bottled	**2 tbsp.**	**30 mL**
Vanilla	**1 1/2 tsp.**	**7 mL**
TOPPING		
Frozen sliced strawberries in syrup (or raspberries), thawed	**15 oz.**	**425 g**
Cornstarch	**1 tbsp.**	**15 mL**

Graham Cracker Crust: Melt butter in saucepan. Stir in graham crumbs and brown sugar. Pack into bottom of ungreased 8 inch (20 cm) springform pan.

Filling: Smooth eggs in blender. Add tofu gradually as you process. Add cheese gradually. Add flour. Process until smooth.

Add sugar, lemon juice and vanilla. Blend. Pour over prepared crust. Bake in 325°F (160°C) oven for about 55 minutes until set.

Topping: Drain juice from strawberries into saucepan. Set strawberries aside.

Stir in cornstarch. Heat and stir until mixture boils and thickens. Cool well. Stir in berries. Spoon over cake wedges. Serves 12.

***1 serving contains:** 305 Calories (1274 kJ); 15.5 g Fat; 10 g Protein; 1 g Fiber*

Don't join their card game. He said he would lead with a club.

PINEAPPLE CRISP

A delicious pudding. A pineapple filling between two layers of oatmeal crumbs.

OATMEAL LAYER		
Hard margarine	**1/3 cup**	**75 mL**
Brown sugar, packed	**1/2 cup**	**125 mL**
Whole wheat flour	**1 cup**	**250 mL**
Rolled oats (not instant)	**1 cup**	**250 mL**
Ground cinnamon	**1/2 tsp.**	**2 mL**
Ground nutmeg	**1/4 tsp.**	**1 mL**
FILLING		
Canned crushed pineapple, with juice	**14 oz.**	**398 mL**
Lemon juice, fresh or bottled	**1 tsp.**	**5 mL**
Brown sugar, packed (optional)	**1/4 cup**	**60 mL**
TOPPING		
Frozen yogurt (or ice cream)	**1 1/2 cups**	**375 mL**

Oatmeal Layer: Melt margarine in saucepan over low heat.

Add brown sugar, flour, rolled oats, cinnamon and nutmeg. Mix until crumbly. Pack 1/2 into bottom of ungreased 1 quart (1 L) casserole.

Filling: Stir pineapple with juice, lemon juice and brown sugar together in separate bowl. Spread over top of oatmeal layer. Cover with remaining 1/2 oatmeal mixture. Bake, uncovered, in 325°F (160°C) oven for about 30 minutes.

Topping: Serve with a dollop of frozen yogurt. Serves 6.

***1 serving contains:** 454 Calories (1901 kJ); 15 g Fat; 8 g Protein; 5 g Fiber*

A haunted wigwam is a creepy teepee.

NATIVE PUDDING

A traditional New England dessert, sometimes called Indian Pudding. This variation takes half as long to bake.

Milk	**2 cups**	**500 mL**
Butter or hard margarine	**1 tbsp.**	**15 mL**
Salt	**1/8 tsp.**	**0.5 mL**
Cornmeal	**1/4 cup**	**60 mL**
Molasses, mild or cooking type	**1/3 cup**	**75 mL**
Raisins (optional)	**1/4 cup**	**60 mL**
Large egg	**1**	**1**
Ground cinnamon	**1/4 tsp.**	**1 mL**
Cream or ice cream		

Scald milk, butter and salt in top of double boiler.

Stir in cornmeal gradually. Cook, stirring occasionally, for about 20 minutes until mixture thickens. Remove from heat.

Combine molasses, raisins, egg and cinnamon in small bowl. Beat well with spoon. Add to cornmeal mixture. Stir. Turn into greased 1 quart (1 L) casserole. Bake, uncovered, in 350°F (175°C) oven for 1 3/4 to 2 hours.

Serve warm with cream or ice cream. Serves 4.

***1 serving contains:** 228 Calories (956 kJ); 7 g Fat; 7 g Protein; 1 g Fiber*

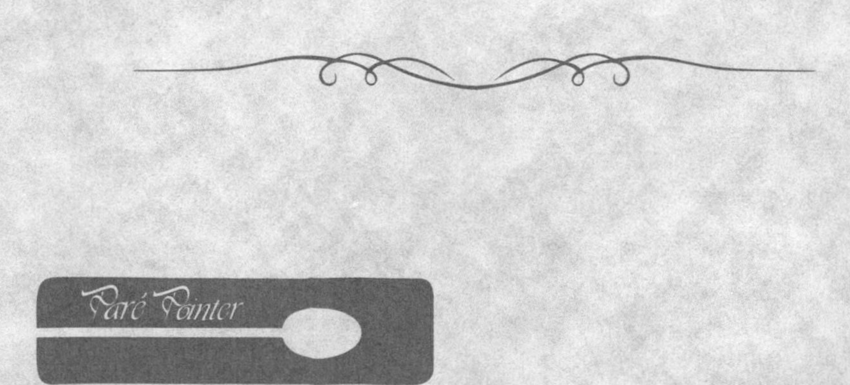

All birds find that flu is common with them.

CUSTARD

This is a good choice to serve for dessert following a vegetable meal.

Large eggs	**3**	**3**
Milk	**2 cups**	**450 mL**
Brown sugar, packed	**¼ cup**	**60 mL**
Salt	**¼ tsp.**	**1 mL**
Vanilla	**1 tsp.**	**5 mL**
Orange flavoring	**¼ tsp.**	**1 mL**
Finely ground pecans (or use cashews for a lighter-colored top)	**⅓ cup**	**75 mL**
Ground nutmeg, sprinkle		

Beat eggs in small bowl until frothy. Add milk, brown sugar, salt, vanilla and orange flavoring. Beat to mix.

Stir in pecans. Pour into ungreased 1 quart (1 L) casserole. Position casserole in center of larger pan with hot water up to within 1 inch (2.5 cm) of top. Bake, uncovered, in 325°F (160°C) oven for about 1 hour. A knife inserted halfway between center and edge should come out clean.

Sprinkle with nutmeg. Serve cold. Serves 4 generously.

1 serving contains: *234 Calories (978 kJ); 11.9 g Fat; 10 g Protein; 1 g Fiber*

GRAHAM BROWNIES

Chewy with lots of chocolate chips.

Graham cracker crumbs	**1 cup**	**250 mL**
Sweetened condensed milk (see Note)	**11 oz.**	**300 mL**
Semisweet chocolate chips	**1 cup**	**250 mL**
Chopped walnuts	**½ cup**	**125 mL**

Measure all ingredients into bowl. Mix well. Pack into greased 8 × 8 inch (20 × 20 cm) pan. Bake in 350°F (175°C) oven for about 25 minutes. Cut while still warm into 25 squares.

Note: If using a 14 oz. (398 mL) can of condensed milk, increase graham cracker crumbs to 1¼ cups (275 mL).

1 square contains: *121 Calories (506 kJ); 6 g Fat; 2 g Protein; 1 g Fiber*

NUTTY CANDY BAR

Full of cereal, peanut butter and peanuts. So good. So rich.

Corn syrup	**1 cup**	**250 mL**
Granulated sugar	**½ cup**	**125 mL**
Smooth peanut butter	**1 cup**	**250 mL**
Vanilla	**1 tsp.**	**5 mL**
Corn flakes cereal	**2 cups**	**500 mL**
Crisp rice cereal	**2 cups**	**500 mL**
Salted peanuts	**1 cup**	**250 mL**
TOPPING		
Semisweet chocolate chips	**2 cups**	**500 mL**
Butter or hard margarine	**¼ cup**	**60 mL**

Heat corn syrup and sugar in large saucepan. Stir to dissolve sugar.

Stir in peanut butter and vanilla.

Add both cereals and peanuts. Stir well. Press into greased 9 × 13 inch (22 × 33 cm) pan. Cool.

Topping: Melt chocolate chips and butter in saucepan over low heat, stirring often. Spread over top. Let stand to harden. Cuts into 54 squares.

1 square contains: *123 Calories (513 kJ); 7.2 g Fat; 2 g Protein; 1 g Fiber*

CRISPY PEANUT BALLS

These need no baking. A nutritious sweet snack.

Smooth peanut butter	**1 cup**	**250 mL**
Liquid honey	**1 cup**	**250 mL**
Skim milk powder	**1 cup**	**250 mL**
Crisp rice cereal	**1 cup**	**250 mL**
Graham cracker crumbs	**¾ cup**	**200 mL**
Granulated sugar	**¼ cup**	**60 mL**

(continued on next page)

Stir peanut butter and honey together well in bowl.

Add milk powder. Mix well.

Add rice cereal and graham crumbs. Stir until mixed. Shape into small balls using about 2 tsp. (10 mL) at a time.

Pour sugar into small bowl. Roll balls in sugar to coat. Best to serve chilled. Makes about 44.

***1 ball contains:** 95 Calories (396 kJ); 3.5 g Fat; 3 g Protein; trace Fiber*

PECAN SQUARES

Pecans rise to the top during baking. When inverted, they are on the bottom.

Butter or hard margarine	**¼ cup**	**60 mL**
All-purpose flour	**⅔ cup**	**150 mL**
Brown sugar, packed	**2 cups**	**500 mL**
Finely chopped pecans	**2 cups**	**500 mL**
Baking soda	**¼ tsp.**	**1 mL**
Salt	**¼ tsp.**	**1 mL**
Large eggs	**4**	**4**
Vanilla	**2 tsp.**	**10 mL**
Icing (confectioner's) sugar, sprinkle		

Melt butter in foil-lined 9 × 13 inch (22 × 33 cm) pan. Set aside.

Combine next 5 ingredients in large bowl. Mix well.

Beat eggs and vanilla in small bowl until volume has increased. Add to flour mixture. Stir. Drop spoonfuls of batter here and there over melted butter. Do not stir. Bake in 350°F (175°C) oven for about 25 minutes. Do not overbake. Remove from oven and immediately invert pan onto tray. Gently remove foil. Cool 30 minutes.

Sift icing sugar over top. Cut when cool. Cuts into 54 squares.

***1 square contains:** 83 Calories (346 kJ); 4.4 g Fat; 1 g Protein; trace Fiber*

BISCUITS WITH HERBS

Eat this flavor-rich biscuit with any main course.

All-purpose flour	**1 cup**	**250 mL**
Whole wheat flour	**1 cup**	**250 mL**
Baking powder	**4 tsp.**	**20 mL**
Salt	**½ tsp.**	**2 mL**
Dill weed	**½ tsp.**	**2 mL**
Ground thyme	**¼ tsp.**	**1 mL**
Garlic powder	**⅛ tsp.**	**0.5 mL**
Granulated sugar	**1 tbsp.**	**15 mL**
Butter or hard margarine	**¼ cup**	**60 mL**
Milk	**¾ cup**	**175 mL**

Measure first 8 ingredients into bowl. Mix well. Cut in butter until crumbly.

Pour milk over top. Stir until mixture forms a soft ball. Knead on lightly floured surface 6 to 8 times. Roll or pat ¾ inch (2 cm) thick. Cut with 2 inch (5 cm) biscuit cutter. Arrange on ungreased baking sheet. Bake in 450°F (230°C) oven for 12 to 15 minutes. Makes 12 biscuits.

1 biscuit contains: *126 Calories (529 kJ); 4.7 g Fat; 3 g Protein; 2 g Fiber*

Pictured on page 143.

APPLE RELISH

A quick relish to make. Crunchy. More dill pickle may be added if desired.

Large cooking apple, with peel, cut up (McIntosh is good)	**1**	**1**
Chopped onion	**2 tbsp.**	**30 mL**
Dill pickle relish or chopped dill pickle	**2 tbsp.**	**30 mL**
Granulated sugar	**2 tbsp.**	**30 mL**
White vinegar	**2 tbsp.**	**30 mL**

Put apple, onion and relish through food grinder or food processor until chunky. Turn into bowl.

Stir in sugar and vinegar. Serve with protein dishes. Makes a generous 1 cup (250 mL).

2 tbsp. (30 mL) contain: *23 Calories (97 kJ); trace Fat; trace Protein; trace Fiber*

ITALIAN CHEESE BREAD

This bread is incredible. One slice is never enough.

All-purpose flour	**2½ cups**	**625 mL**
Granulated sugar	**¼ cup**	**60 mL**
Envelopes active dry yeast	**2 × ¼ oz.**	**2 × 8 g**
Salt	**1½ tsp.**	**7 mL**
Milk	**1 cup**	**250 mL**
Water	**1 cup**	**250 ml**
Butter or hard margarine	**½ cup**	**125 mL**
Large eggs	**2**	**2**
All-purpose flour, approximately	**2¾ cups**	**675 mL**
FILLING		
Grated mozzarella cheese	**1 cup**	**250 mL**
Butter or hard margarine, softened	**¼ cup**	**60 mL**
Envelope Italian dressing and dip mix (such as Salads 'N Dips)	**1½ oz.**	**42 g**
Garlic powder	**¼ tsp.**	**1 mL**
Sesame seeds	**2 tbsp.**	**30 mL**

Place first 4 ingredients in large bowl. Stir well.

Heat milk, water and butter in saucepan until quite warm and butter is melted. Add to yeast mixture.

Add eggs. Beat on low to moisten. Beat on medium for 3 minutes.

Work in enough remaining flour to make stiff batter.

Filling: Mix first 4 ingredients well in small bowl.

Grease 12 cup (2.7 L) bundt pan well. Sprinkle with sesame seeds. Spoon half of batter into pan. Spoon filling over top keeping it about ½ inch (12 mm) from sides. Spoon remaining batter over filling. Cover with greased waxed paper and tea towel. Let rise in oven with light on and door closed for about 30 minutes until doubled in size. Bake in 350°F (175°C) oven for about 30 minutes until golden brown. Bread will sound hollow when tapped with knuckle. Immediately remove from pan to rack to cool. Serve warm or cold. Makes 1 loaf that cuts into 24 delectable slices.

***1 slice contains:** 208 Calories (870 kJ); 8.8 g Fat; 6 g Protein; 1 g Fiber*

RED ONION SALSA

Colorful and chunky. This is spicy hot and very good. A good go-with for protein dishes.

Large red onion, chopped	**1**	**1**
Red pepper, chopped	**1**	**1**
Red wine vinegar	**1/4 cup**	**60 mL**
Instant vegetable stock mix	**1 tbsp.**	**15 mL**
Ground thyme	**1/4 tsp.**	**1 mL**
Salt	**1/2 tsp.**	**2 mL**
Pepper	**1/8 tsp.**	**0.5 mL**
Cayenne pepper	**1/8 tsp.**	**0.5 mL**

Combine all ingredients in saucepan. Bring to a boil over medium heat. Continue to boil slowly, stirring occasionally, until thickened. This will take about 20 minutes. Cool. Makes 1 1/2 cups (350 mL).

2 tbsp. (30 mL) contain: *12 Calories (52 kJ); trace Fat; trace Protein; trace Fiber*

Pictured on page 35.

ALMOND BISCUITS

Light and tender. You are getting extra protein without knowing it.

All-purpose flour	**2 cups**	**500 mL**
Ground almonds	**1/2 cup**	**125 mL**
Granulated sugar	**2 tbsp.**	**30 mL**
Baking powder	**4 tsp.**	**20 mL**
Salt	**3/4 tsp.**	**4 mL**
Cooking oil	**1/3 cup**	**75 mL**
Milk	**3/4 cup**	**175 mL**

Stir first 5 ingredients together in bowl.

Add cooking oil and milk. Stir to form a soft ball. Knead on lightly floured surface 6 to 8 times. Roll or pat 3/4 inch (2 cm) thick. Cut with 2 inch (5 cm) biscuit cutter. Arrange on ungreased baking sheet. Bake in 450°F (230°C) oven for 12 to 15 minutes. Makes 12 biscuits.

1 biscuit contains: *179 Calories (749 kJ); 9.1 g Fat; 4 g Protein; 1 g Fiber*

MANGO CHUTNEY

Ideal to serve with recipes high in protein. Bright and colorful.

Ripe firm mango, peeled and cut in small pieces	**1**	**1**
White vinegar	**1/4 cup**	**60 mL**
Brown sugar, packed	**1/4 cup**	**60 mL**
Raisins, coarsely chopped	**1/3 cup**	**75 mL**
Prepared mustard	**1 tsp.**	**5 mL**
Ground ginger	**1/4 tsp.**	**1 mL**
Garlic powder	**1/8 tsp.**	**0.5 mL**
Hot pepper sauce	**1/8 tsp.**	**0.5 mL**

Combine all ingredients in heavy saucepan. Stir. Bring to a boil. Cover. Simmer slowly, stirring often, for about 15 minutes until mango is tender. Makes 1 1/4 cups (300 mL).

2 tbsp. (30 mL) contain: *46 Calories (193 kJ); trace Fat; trace Protein; 1 g Fiber*

NUTTY RAISIN BREAD

Try this instead of regular bread. Good toasted, too.

Large egg	**1**	**1**
Milk	**1 cup**	**250 mL**
Cooking oil	**1 tbsp.**	**15 mL**
Coarsely chopped raisins	**1 cup**	**250 mL**
Chopped walnuts	**1 cup**	**250 mL**
All-purpose flour	**1 1/2 cups**	**375 mL**
Whole wheat flour	**1 1/2 cups**	**375 mL**
Baking powder	**1 tbsp.**	**15 mL**
Salt	**1 tsp.**	**5 mL**

Beat egg in bowl. Add milk, cooking oil, raisins and walnuts.

Add remaining ingredients. Stir to moisten. Dough will be stiff. Turn into greased 9 x 5 x 3 inch (22 x 12 x 7 cm) loaf pan. Pat top smooth. Let stand 20 minutes at room temperature. Bake in 350°F (175°C) oven for about 40 minutes. Cool for 10 minutes. Turn out onto rack. Makes 1 loaf, 12 slices.

1 slice contains: *251 Calories (1052 kJ); 9.3 g Fat; 7 g Protein; 4 g Fiber*

RAISIN WHEAT MUFFINS

Contain raisins and walnuts. Moist and tasty.

Large eggs	**2**	**2**
Cooking oil	**2 tbsp.**	**30 mL**
Sour milk (or 1 tbsp., 15 mL, white vinegar plus milk)	**1 cup**	**250 mL**
Baking soda	**½ tsp.**	**2 mL**
Raisins	**½ cup**	**125 mL**
Chopped walnuts	**⅓ cup**	**75 mL**
All-purpose flour	**1 cup**	**250 mL**
Whole wheat flour	**1 cup**	**250 mL**
Brown sugar, packed	**¼ cup**	**60 mL**
Baking powder	**2 tsp.**	**10 mL**
Salt	**½ tsp.**	**2 mL**

Beat eggs in bowl. Add cooking oil.

Stir sour milk and baking soda together to dissolve baking soda. Add to egg mixture.

Add raisins and walnuts. Stir.

Stir remaining ingredients together in separate bowl. Add to batter. Stir to moisten. Fill greased muffin cups almost full. Bake in 400°F (205°C) oven for about 15 minutes until an inserted wooden pick comes out clean. Let stand 5 minutes. Remove to rack to cool. Makes 12 muffins.

1 muffin contains: *181 Calories (759 kJ); 6.2 g Fat; 5 g Protein; 2 g Fiber*

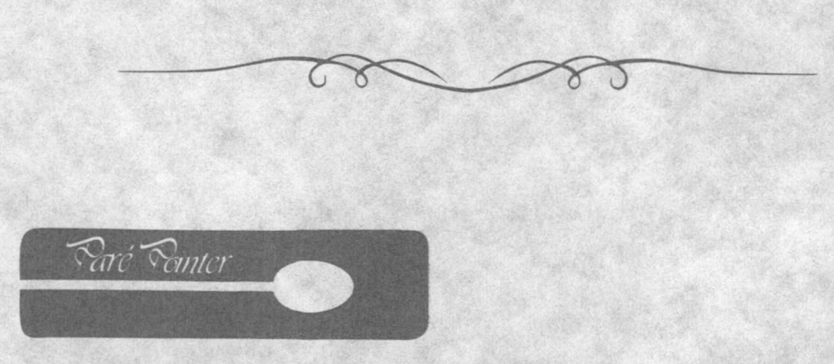

When young Havie was asked to use the words "defeat", "defence", and "detail" in a sentence he replied, "Defeat went over defence before detail".

TAHINI

This sesame spread works well on its own or in recipes such as Hummus, page 12 or Tahini Sauce, page 130.

Sesame seeds	**½ cup**	**125 mL**
Water	**¼ cup**	**60 mL**
Cooking oil	**2 tbsp.**	**30 mL**

Spread sesame seeds in ungreased jelly roll pan or larger pan. Toast in 350°F (175°C) oven for 5 to 10 minutes. Stir seeds every 2 minutes. The idea is to brown, not blacken, seeds. Place in blender.

Add water and cooking oil. Process about 3 minutes until smooth. Makes ½ cup (125 mL).

1 tbsp. (15 mL) contains: *83 Calories (348 kJ); 7.9 g Fat; 2 g Protein; 2 g Fiber*

PEANUT LOAF

There is a faint hint of peanut butter. Moist and flavorful.

Boiling water	**1 cup**	**250 mL**
Instant rice	**1 cup**	**250 mL**
Canned tomatoes with juice, mashed	**1 cup**	**250 mL**
Ground (or finely grated) carrot	**1 cup**	**250 mL**
Finely chopped onion	**¼ cup**	**60 mL**
Ground (or finely grated) potato	**1 cup**	**250 mL**
Soda cracker crumbs	**1 cup**	**250 mL**
Bulgur	**½ cup**	**125 mL**
Smooth peanut butter	**⅓ cup**	**75 mL**
Large egg	**1**	**1**
Salt	**½ tsp.**	**2 mL**
Pepper	**¼ tsp.**	**1 mL**
Ketchup	**3 tbsp.**	**50 mL**

Combine boiling water and rice. Let stand 5 minutes.

Measure next 10 ingredients into bowl. Mix well. Add rice. Stir. Pack into greased 8 x 4 x 3 inch (20 x 10 x 7 cm) loaf pan.

Spread ketchup over top. Bake, uncovered, in 350°F (175°C) oven for about 1 hour. Cuts into 8 slices.

1 slice contains: *238 Calories (996 kJ); 7.9 g Fat; 8 g Protein; 4 g Fiber*

VEGETABLE CUTLETS

Look like small browned steaks. Good, with a mild flavor.

Canned mixed vegetables, drained (corn, green beans and carrot)	**2 × 14 oz.**	**2 × 398 mL**
Cooked mashed potato	**1 cup**	**250 mL**
Canned pinto beans, drained	**14 oz.**	**398 mL**
Large eggs	**2**	**2**
Large shredded wheat biscuits, crushed	**4**	**4**
Salt	**1 tsp.**	**5 mL**
Pepper	**¼ tsp.**	**1 mL**
Onion powder	**1 tsp.**	**5 mL**
Grated medium or sharp Cheddar cheese	**½ cup**	**125 mL**
Fine dry bread crumbs	**1 cup**	**250 mL**
Cooking oil	**1 tbsp.**	**15 mL**

Mash first 3 ingredients in food processor or with a fork. Turn into bowl.

Mix in next 7 ingredients. Let stand 10 minutes. Shape into ½ cup (125 mL) cutlets (patties).

Heat cooking oil in frying pan. Add cutlets. Brown both sides. Add more cooking oil as needed. Makes 10 cutlets.

1 cutlet contains: *211 Calories (885 kJ); 5.3 g Fat; 9 g Protein; 5 g Fiber*

Pictured on page 71.

Sign on a pest controller's door: We gladly make mouse calls.

STRAW AND HAY

Make with colored fettuccine that matches the colors of straw and hay. Includes peas and "meat" strips.

Green fettuccine	**8 oz.**	**250 g**
Boiling water	**3 qts.**	**3 L**
Cooking oil (optional)	**1 tbsp.**	**15 mL**
Salt	**2 tsp.**	**10 mL**
White fettuccine	**8 oz.**	**250 g**
Boiling water	**3 qts.**	**3 L**
Cooking oil (optional)	**1 tbsp.**	**15 mL**
Salt	**2 tsp.**	**10 mL**
Butter or hard margarine	**2 tbsp.**	**30 mL**
Sliced fresh mushrooms	**2 cups**	**500 mL**
Skim evaporated milk (or whipping cream)	**13½ oz.**	**385 mL**
Frozen peas	**2 cups**	**500 mL**
Salt	**½ tsp.**	**2 mL**
Pepper	**¼ tsp.**	**1 mL**
Garlic powder	**¼ tsp.**	**1 mL**
Veggie deli slices, cut in short strips	**5½ oz.**	**155 g**
Grated Parmesan cheese	**¼ cup**	**60 mL**
Grated Parmesan cheese	**¼ cup**	**60 mL**

Cook green fettuccine in large uncovered pot in first amounts of boiling water, cooking oil and salt for 9 to 11 minutes until tender but firm. Drain. Return fettuccine to pot.

Cook white fettuccine in separate large uncovered pot in second amounts of boiling water, cooking oil and salt for 5 to 7 minutes until tender but firm. Drain. Add white fettuccine to green fettuccine in pot.

Melt butter in frying pan. Add mushrooms. Sauté until soft.

Stir in milk and peas. Cover and simmer for 2 to 3 minutes to cook peas. Add to fettuccine.

Add third amount of salt, pepper, garlic powder, deli strips and first amount of Parmesan cheese. Heat until piping hot. Turn into serving bowl or platter.

Sprinkle with second amount of Parmesan cheese. Makes 12 cups (3 L).

2 cups (500 mL) contain: *532 Calories (2211 kJ); 8.5 g Fat; 31 g Protein; 9 g Fiber*

MEAL IN A DISH

Talk about variety! Add a dinner roll and a salad for a real spread.

Chopped onion	**1 cup**	**250 mL**
Chopped celery	**1 cup**	**250 mL**
Diced yellow turnip	**1 cup**	**250 mL**
Diced potato	**1 cup**	**250 mL**
Diced carrot	**1 cup**	**250 mL**
Diced parsnip	**1 cup**	**250 mL**
Dried red lentils	**1 cup**	**250 mL**
Boiling water	**2 cups**	**500 mL**
Smooth peanut butter	**1/4 cup**	**60 mL**
Salt	**1/2 tsp.**	**2 mL**
Pepper	**1/8 tsp.**	**0.5 mL**

Place first 7 ingredients in ungreased 3 quart (3 L) casserole. Stir to mix evenly.

Stir boiling water and peanut butter together. Add salt and pepper. Stir. Pour over vegetables. Cover. Bake in 350°F (175°C) oven for 1 1/4 to 1 1/2 hours until vegetables are tender. Serves 6.

1 serving contains: *258 Calories (1081 kJ); 6.3 g Fat; 14 g Protein; 6 g Fiber*

Pictured on page 53.

1. Veggie Stir-Fry, page 146
2. Rice Veggie Casserole, page 73
3. Noodle Casserole, page 58 with Tofu Sausages, page 74
4. Meal In A Dish, page 52

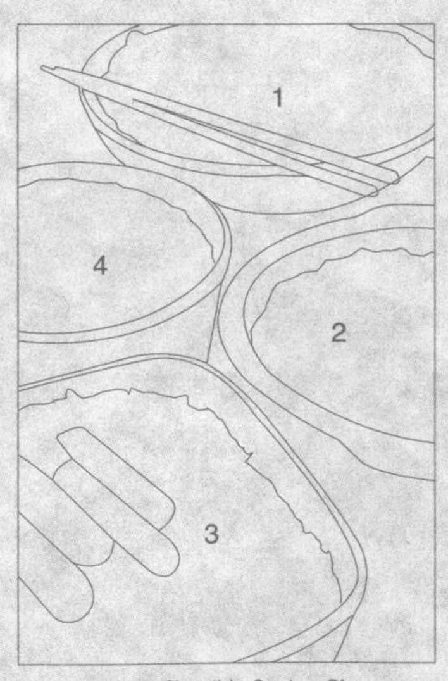

Casserole Dishes Courtesy Of:
The Bay Housewares Dept.

Napkins Courtesy Of:
La Cache

Wok Courtesy Of:
Eaton's Housewares Dept.

Tablecloth Courtesy Of:
Creations By Design

Chopsticks Courtesy Of:
Enchanted Kitchen

MEATLESS MOUSSAKA

Looks and tastes just like moussaka that contains meat.

Medium eggplants, peeled and sliced ¼ inch (6 mm) thick	**3**	**3**
Salt, sprinkle		
SAUCE		
Butter or hard margarine	**2 tbsp.**	**30 mL**
Frozen sliced mushrooms (or 2 lbs., 1 kg, fresh sliced)	**2 lbs.**	**1 kg**
Chopped onion	**1½ cups**	**375 mL**
Tomato paste	**5½ oz.**	**156 mL**
Garlic powder	**½ tsp.**	**2 mL**
Sweet basil	**½ tsp.**	**2 mL**
Whole oregano	**½ tsp.**	**2 mL**
Granulated sugar	**½ tsp.**	**2 mL**
Salt	**¾ tsp.**	**4 mL**
Pepper	**¼ tsp.**	**1 mL**
Ground cinnamon, scant measure	**¼ tsp.**	**1 mL**
Grated mozzarella cheese	**2 cups**	**500 mL**
Grated Parmesan cheese	**1 tbsp.**	**15 mL**

Arrange eggplant slices on ungreased baking sheet. Sprinkle with salt. Bake in 375°F (190°C) oven for about 5 minutes until tender.

Sauce: Melt butter in frying pan. Sauté ½ of mushrooms until soft, then second ½, then onion, adding more butter as needed. Remove to large bowl as each batch is finished.

Add next 8 ingredients. Stir.

Assemble in greased 9 x 9 inch (22 x 22 cm) pan in layers as follows:

1. ½ eggplant slices
2. ½ sauce
3. ½ eggplant slices
4. ½ sauce
5. Mozzarella cheese
6. Parmesan cheese

Bake, uncovered, in 350°F (175°C) oven for about 30 minutes. Serves 6.

1 serving contains: *260 Calories (1087 kJ); 14.3 g Fat; 15 g Protein; 6 g Fiber*

LAZY LASAGNE

A soft, reddish filling with a golden topping and a lasagne flavor, too. No noodles in this.

Creamed cottage cheese	**1 cup**	**250 mL**
"Meat" Scramble, page 96	**1 cup**	**250 mL**
Tomato paste	**5½ oz.**	**156 mL**
Grated mozzarella cheese	**½ cup**	**125 mL**
Whole oregano	**½ tsp.**	**2 mL**
Salt	**½ tsp.**	**2 mL**
Chopped chives	**2 tsp.**	**10 mL**
Granulated sugar	**½ tsp.**	**2 mL**
All-purpose flour	**½ cup**	**125 mL**
Baking powder	**1 tsp.**	**5 mL**
Salt	**¼ tsp.**	**1 mL**
Cooking oil	**1 tbsp.**	**15 mL**
Large eggs	**2**	**2**
Milk	**1 cup**	**250 mL**

Spread cottage cheese in greased 8 x 8 inch (20 x 20 cm) pan.

Mix next 7 ingredients well in bowl. Spoon over cottage cheese.

Stir flour, baking powder and salt together in bowl. Beat in cooking oil and eggs. Add milk. Beat to mix. Pour over all. Bake in 400°F (205°C) oven for 40 to 45 minutes until a knife inserted in center comes out clean. Cuts into 6 servings.

1 serving contains: *262 Calories (1095 kJ); 9.8 g Fat; 16 g Protein; 4 g Fiber*

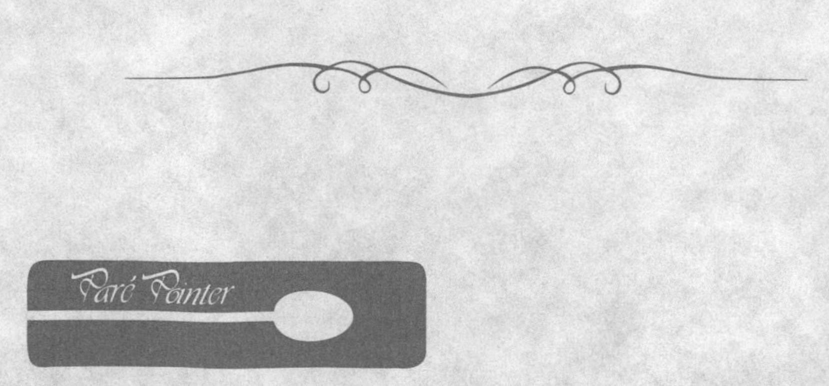

When everything is coming your way, better check what lane you're in.

CHEESY RICE

Makes a large layered casserole. Great flavor.

Brown rice	**2 cups**	**500 mL**
Boiling water	**4 cups**	**1 L**
Salt	**1 tsp.**	**5 mL**
Butter or hard margarine	**1½ tbsp.**	**25 mL**
Chopped onion	**1½ cups**	**375 mL**
Canned black-eyed peas, drained	**14 oz.**	**398 mL**
Canned chopped green chilies	**4 oz.**	**114 mL**
Garlic powder	**½ tsp.**	**2 mL**
Parsley flakes	**1 tsp.**	**5 mL**
Pepper	**¼ tsp.**	**1 mL**
Grated Monterey Jack cheese	**2 cups**	**500 mL**
Creamed cottage cheese	**2 cups**	**500 mL**
Grated medium or sharp Cheddar cheese	**¾ cup**	**175 mL**

Cook rice in boiling water with salt for about 45 minutes until tender and water is absorbed.

Melt butter in frying pan. Add onion. Sauté until soft. Add to rice.

Add peas, green chilies, garlic powder, parsley and pepper. Stir.

Assemble in layers in ungreased 3 quart (3 L) casserole as follows:

1. ⅓ rice mixture
2. ½ Monterey Jack cheese
3. ½ cottage cheese
4. ⅓ rice mixture
5. ½ Monterey Jack cheese
6. ½ cottage cheese
7. ⅓ rice mixture
8. Cheddar cheese

Bake, covered, in 350°F (175°C) oven for about 1 hour until heated through and cheese is melted. If you would like to brown cheese a little, remove cover and bake 10 minutes more. Serves 8.

1 serving contains: *482 Calories (2018 kJ); 19.7 g Fat; 25 g Protein; 6 g Fiber*

NOODLE CASSEROLE

A large casserole. Tomato adds color. Good flavor.

Medium egg noodles	**1 lb.**	**454 g**
Boiling water	**4 qts.**	**4 L**
Cooking oil (optional)	**1 tbsp.**	**15 mL**
Salt	**1 tbsp.**	**15 mL**
Cooking oil	**1½ tbsp.**	**25 mL**
Chopped onion	**1¼ cups**	**300 mL**
Green pepper, chopped	**1**	**1**
Sausages, sliced (see Note)	**8**	**8**
Canned stewed tomatoes	**14 oz.**	**398 mL**
Condensed tomato soup	**10 oz.**	**284 mL**
Canned sliced mushrooms, drained	**10 oz.**	**284 mL**
Grated Parmesan cheese	**⅓ cup**	**75 mL**

Cook egg noodles in boiling water, first amount of cooking oil and salt in large uncovered saucepan for 5 to 7 minutes until tender but firm. Drain. Return noodles to saucepan.

Heat second amount of cooking oil in frying pan. Add onion and green pepper. Sauté until soft. Add to noodles in saucepan.

Add sausage, tomatoes, soup and mushrooms. Stir. Turn into ungreased 3 quart (3 L) casserole.

Sprinkle with cheese. Bake, covered, in 350°F (175°C) oven for about 30 minutes. Remove cover. Bake 5 minutes more. Serves 8.

Note: Use either Tofu Sausages, page 74 or White Bean Sausages, page 76.

1 serving contains: *385 Calories (1612 kJ); 10.5 g Fat; 16 g Protein; 5 g Fiber*

Pictured on page 53.

Paré Pointer

Little Mary knew a train just went by because she could see its tracks.

VEGGIE STEW

A potful of beans and vegetables. Add spices to suit your taste.

Canned kidney beans, drained and liquid reserved	**14 oz.**	**398 mL**
Canned small white beans, drained and liquid reserved	**19 oz.**	**540 mL**
Canned chick peas (garbanzo beans), drained and liquid reserved	**19 oz.**	**540 mL**
Reserved liquids		
Water	**1 cup**	**250 mL**
Medium potatoes, cubed	**2**	**2**
Medium carrots, cubed	**2**	**2**
Cubed turnip	**1 cup**	**250 mL**
Chopped onion	**2 cups**	**500 mL**
Grated cabbage, packed	**1 cup**	**250 mL**
Thinly sliced celery	**1/2 cup**	**125 mL**
Soy sauce	**2 tbsp.**	**30 mL**
Bay leaves	**2**	**2**
Instant vegetable stock mix	**2 tsp.**	**10 mL**
Garlic powder	**1/4-1 tsp.**	**1-5 mL**
Ground thyme	**1/4-1 tsp.**	**1-5 mL**
Ground marjoram	**1/4-1 tsp.**	**1-5 mL**
Ground cumin	**1/8-1/4 tsp.**	**0.5-1 mL**
Salt	**1 tsp.**	**5 mL**
Pepper	**1/4 tsp.**	**1 mL**
Canned stewed tomatoes, mashed	**14 oz.**	**398 mL**
Peas, fresh or frozen	**1 cup**	**250 mL**
Cornstarch	**3 tbsp.**	**50 mL**
Water	**3 tbsp.**	**50 mL**

Combine beans in medium bowl. Set aside.

Combine next 17 ingredients in Dutch oven using least quantity of seasonings. Cover and simmer for 10 minutes. Add beans. Continue to simmer about 3 minutes more until vegetables are tender-crisp.

Add tomatoes and peas. Boil 3 to 4 minutes. Taste. Add more seasoning if desired.

Stir cornstarch into last amount of water in small cup. Stir into boiling stew until it returns to a boil and thickens slightly. Discard bay leaves. Makes 12 cups (3 L).

***2 cups (500 mL) contain:** 397 Calories (1659 kJ); 3.1 g Fat; 20 g Protein; 14 g Fiber*

SAUCED PASTA

A creamy egg and asparagus sauce tops the pasta. Adds a wonderful flavor.

Fusilli pasta (spiral)	**4 cups**	**1 L**
Boiling water	**3 qts.**	**3 L**
Cooking oil (optional)	**1 tbsp.**	**15 mL**
Salt	**1 tbsp.**	**15 mL**
SAUCE		
All-purpose flour	**6 tbsp.**	**100 mL**
Salt	**1 tsp.**	**5 mL**
Pepper	**¼ tsp.**	**1 mL**
Onion powder	**¼ tsp.**	**1 mL**
Skim evaporated milk	**1½ cups**	**375 mL**
Milk	**1½ cups**	**375 mL**
Butter or hard margarine	**1 tbsp.**	**15 mL**
Hard-boiled eggs, cut lengthwise into 8 thin wedges	**2-4**	**2-4**
Canned asparagus pieces, drained	**12 oz.**	**341 mL**

Cook fusilli in boiling water, cooking oil and salt in large uncovered pot for 10 to 12 minutes until tender but firm. Drain.

Sauce: Stir flour, salt, pepper and onion powder together in saucepan. Gradually stir in evaporated milk, ensuring there are no lumps. Stir in remaining milk. Heat and stir until sauce boils and thickens.

Stir in butter.

Add eggs and asparagus. Heat, stirring gently, until hot. Divide fusilli among 4 plates. Spoon sauce over each. Serves 4.

***1 serving contains:** 593 Calories (2481 kJ); 11 g Fat; 28 g Protein; 4 g Fiber*

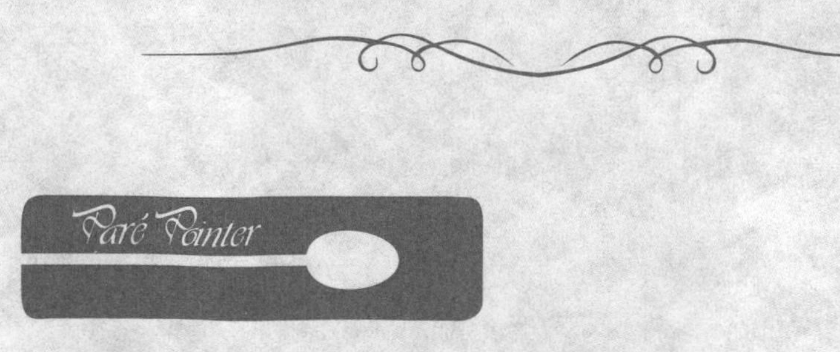

He was running to stop a fight. It was between him and another fellow.

BROCCOLI RICE BAKE

Both convenient and simple to make.

Butter or hard margarine	**1 tbsp.**	**15 mL**
Chopped onion	**½ cup**	**125 mL**
Chopped celery	**¼ cup**	**60 mL**
Broccoli, coarsely chopped	**1 lb.**	**454 g**
Boiling water		
Condensed cream of mushroom soup	**10 oz.**	**284 mL**
Soup can of water	**10 oz.**	**284 mL**
Soup can of instant rice	**10 oz.**	**284 mL**
Grated medium or sharp Cheddar cheese	**½ cup**	**125 mL**
Worcestershire sauce	**1 tsp.**	**5 mL**
Ground thyme	**⅛ tsp.**	**0.5 mL**
Cayenne pepper	**⅛ tsp.**	**0.5 mL**
Grated medium or sharp Cheddar cheese	**¼ cup**	**60 mL**

Melt butter in frying pan. Add onion and celery. Sauté until soft.

Cook broccoli in boiling water until tender-crisp. Drain.

Mix next 7 ingredients in a large bowl. Add vegetables. Stir. Turn into ungreased 2 quart (2 L) casserole.

Sprinkle with remaining cheese. Cover. Bake in 350°F (175°C) oven for 30 to 35 minutes. Serves 6.

1 serving contains: *232 Calories (969 kJ); 11.1 g Fat; 7 g Protein; 3 g Fiber*

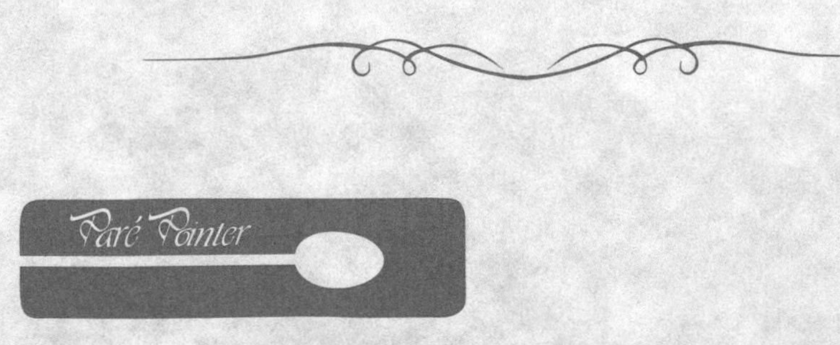

It was a good thing retreads were invented for people who retire.

EASY LASAGNE

Simple to prepare. You won't miss the meat.

SAUCE		
Butter or hard margarine	**1½ tbsp.**	**25 mL**
Sliced fresh mushrooms	**1½ cups**	**375 mL**
Chopped onion	**1 cup**	**250 mL**
Pasta sauce, preferably chunky, with garlic and onion	**25 oz.**	**700 mL**
Mild salsa	**1 cup**	**250 mL**
CHEESE FILLING		
Egg white (large)	**1**	**1**
Low-fat cottage cheese (less than 1% MF)	**1 cup**	**250 mL**
Grated Parmesan cheese	**½ cup**	**125 mL**
Oven-ready lasagne noodles	**6**	**6**
Grated part-skim mozzarella cheese (35% less fat)	**1½ cups**	**375 mL**
Grated Parmesan cheese	**¼ cup**	**60 mL**

Sauce: Melt butter in large saucepan. Add mushrooms and onion. Sauté until soft.

Add pasta sauce and salsa. Simmer, stirring often, for about 3 minutes. Remove from heat.

Cheese Filling: Mix egg white, cottage cheese and first amount of Parmesan cheese in small bowl. Set aside.

Assemble in ungreased 9 x 9 inch (22 x 22 cm) pan in layers as follows:

1. ⅓ cup sauce
2. 3 lasagne noodles
3. ½ cheese filling
4. ½ remaining sauce
5. ½ mozzarella cheese
6. 3 lasagne noodles
7. ½ cheese filling
8. Remaining sauce
9. Remaining mozzarella cheese
10. Parmesan cheese

Bake, covered, in 350°F (175°C) oven for about 45 minutes. Uncover. Bake 10 to 15 minutes more. Let stand 10 minutes before serving. Serves 6.

***1 serving contains:** 304 Calories (1272 kJ); 13.4 g Fat; 23 g Protein; 4 g Fiber*

BROCCOLI PASTA CASSEROLE

Broccoli is sandwiched between layers of noodles. Cheese topping adds flavor as well as color.

Broad noodles	**½ lb.**	**227 g**
Boiling water	**3 qts.**	**3 L**
Cooking oil (optional)	**1 tbsp.**	**15 mL**
Salt	**2 tsp.**	**10 mL**
Broccoli, 1 bunch, cut up (about ¾ lb., 375 g)	**4 cups**	**1 L**
Boiling water	**1 cup**	**250 mL**
Salt	**¼ tsp.**	**1 mL**
Large eggs	**2**	**2**
Creamed cottage cheese	**1 cup**	**250 mL**
Plain yogurt	**½ cup**	**125 mL**
Salt	**¾ tsp.**	**4 mL**
Grated medium or sharp Cheddar cheese	**½ cup**	**125 mL**

Cook noodles in first amount of boiling water, cooking oil and salt in large uncovered saucepan for 6 to 10 minutes until tender but firm. Drain. Put ½ noodles in greased 2 quart (2 L) casserole.

Cook broccoli in second amount of boiling water and salt until tender-crisp. Drain. Spread over noodles in casserole.

Combine eggs, cottage cheese, yogurt and salt in blender. Process until smooth. Pour ½ over broccoli. Cover with remaining noodles.

Sprinkle with cheese. Pour remaining egg mixture over all. Bake, covered, in 350°F (175°C) oven for about 20 minutes. Remove cover. Bake 10 minutes more until bubbly hot. Serves 6.

1 serving contains: *281 Calories (1175 kJ); 8.1 g Fat; 18 g Protein; 2 g Fiber*

Paré Pointer

He who says he is too old to learn anything new probably always was.

MACARONI AND CHEESE

Such a satisfying dish. Crumb topping adds the finish.

Elbow macaroni	**1½ cups**	**375 mL**
Boiling water	**3 qts.**	**3 L**
Cooking oil (optional)	**1 tbsp.**	**15 mL**
Salt	**2 tsp.**	**10 mL**
Butter or hard margarine	**1 tbsp.**	**15 mL**
Finely chopped onion	**½ cup**	**125 mL**
Condensed cream of mushroom soup	**10 oz.**	**284 mL**
Milk	**⅔ cup**	**150 mL**
Salt	**½ tsp.**	**2 mL**
Pepper, sprinkle		
Grated medium Cheddar cheese	**2 cups**	**500 mL**
TOPPING		
Butter or hard margarine	**2 tbsp.**	**30 mL**
Dry bread crumbs	**½ cup**	**125 mL**
Grated medium Cheddar cheese	**¼ cup**	**60 mL**

Cook macaroni in boiling water, cooking oil and salt in large uncovered saucepan for 5 to 7 minutes until tender but firm. Drain. Return macaroni to saucepan.

Heat butter in frying pan. Add onion. Sauté until soft.

Stir in soup, milk, salt, pepper and cheese until mixed and cheese is melted. Add to macaroni. Stir. Turn into greased 1½ quart (1.5 L) casserole.

Topping: Melt butter in separate saucepan. Remove from heat. Add bread crumbs. Stir until mixed. Add cheese. Stir. Spread over casserole. Bake, uncovered, in 350°F (175°C) oven for about 30 minutes until browned and bubbly hot. Serves 6.

1 serving contains: *468 Calories (1958 kJ); 28.0 g Fat; 19 g Protein; 1 g Fiber*

Paré Pointer

When you introduce one strawberry to another, you have a strawberry shake.

BEAN-SAUCED PASTA

A meal in one plateful.

TOMATO BEAN SAUCE		
Cooking oil	1 tbsp.	15 mL
Chopped onion	1 cup	250 mL
Small green pepper, seeded and chopped	1	1
Garlic clove, minced (or 1/4 tsp., 1 mL, garlic powder)	1	1
Canned stewed tomatoes, broken up	14 oz.	398 mL
Canned kidney beans, drained	14 oz.	398 mL
Apple juice	1/2 cup	125 mL
Salt	1/4 tsp.	1 mL
Pepper	1/8 tsp.	0.5 mL
Liquid smoke	1/8-1/4 tsp.	0.5-1 mL
PASTA		
Rigatoni or penne (tube pasta)	1 lb.	454 g
Boiling water	4 qts.	4 L
Cooking oil (optional)	1 tbsp.	15 mL
Salt	1 tbsp.	15 mL

Tomato Bean Sauce: Heat cooking oil in frying pan. Add onion, green pepper and garlic. Sauté until soft.

Add tomatoes, kidney beans, apple juice, salt and pepper. Stir. Add lesser amount of liquid smoke. Stir and taste. Add more if desired. Boil slowly for about 30 minutes until mixture gets slightly thicker.

Pasta: Cook rigatoni in boiling water, cooking oil and salt in large uncovered pot for 11 to 13 minutes until tender but firm. Drain. Divide among 4 warm plates. Divide sauce over top. Serves 4.

1 serving contains: *605 Calories (2530 kJ); 5.9 g Fat; 22 g Protein; 12 g Fiber*

Paré Pointer

Nowadays a hot school lunch isn't a warm meal. It's a stolen sandwich.

DHAL

Good.

The sauce is made with lentils and served over a bed of rice.

Red lentils	**1 cup**	**250 mL**
Water	**2 cups**	**500 mL**
Chopped onion	**1 cup**	**250 mL**
Large tomato, diced	**1**	**1**
Garlic cloves, minced (or ½ tsp., 2 mL garlic powder)	**2**	**2**
Turmeric	**¼ tsp.**	**1 mL**
Cayenne pepper	**½-1 tsp.**	**2-5 mL**
Salt	**¾ tsp.**	**4 mL**
Ground coriander	**1 tsp.**	**5 mL**
Basmati rice	**1⅓ cups**	**325 mL**
Water	**2⅔ cups**	**650 mL**
Salt	**½ tsp.**	**2 mL**

Measure first 9 ingredients into saucepan. Cover. Cook for about 20 minutes until vegetables are tender. Cool. Run through blender, or if you like, serve as is.

Cook rice in water and second amount of salt for about 15 minutes until tender and moisture is absorbed. Pour lentil mixture over each serving of rice. Serves 6.

1 serving contains: *291 Calories (1217 kJ); 0.8 g Fat; 13 g Protein; 6 g Fiber*

ZUCCHINI DHAL

A complete dish with lentils, zucchini and rice.

Mung dhal (split mung beans)	**1 cup**	**250 mL**
Water	**3 cups**	**750 mL**
Salt	**1 tsp.**	**5 mL**
Medium zucchini with skin, chopped (about 4 cups, 1 L)	**2**	**2**
Coconut powder (or fine coconut)	**2 tbsp.**	**30 mL**
Cooking oil	**1 tsp.**	**5 mL**
Cumin seeds	**¼ tsp.**	**1 mL**
Cayenne pepper (add more to taste)	**⅛ tsp.**	**0.5 mL**
Basmati rice (or other long grain rice)	**1½ cups**	**375 mL**
Water	**3 cups**	**750 mL**
Salt	**½ tsp.**	**2 mL**

(continued on next page)

Combine mung dhal, water and first amount of salt in saucepan. Bring to a boil. Cover. Simmer for about 25 minutes until soft.

Add zucchini and coconut powder. Simmer for 5 to 10 minutes until zucchini is soft.

Stir cooking oil, cumin seeds and cayenne in small pan. Fry quickly and add to zucchini mixture.

Simmer rice, covered, in water and second amount of salt for about 15 minutes until tender and water is absorbed. Serve dhal alongside or over rice. Serves 8.

1 serving contains: *249 Calories (1040 kJ); 2.1 g Fat; 10 g Protein; 4 g Fiber*

CURRY BEAN BAKE

Dark with a mild curry flavor. Increase amount of curry to suit taste. Easy to double recipe.

Canned kidney beans, with liquid, ground or mashed	**14 oz.**	**398 mL**
Ground walnuts (or other nuts)	**1 cup**	**250 mL**
Large eggs, beaten	**3**	**3**
Ketchup	**3 tbsp.**	**50 mL**
Curry powder	**½ tsp.**	**2 mL**
Ground sage	**½ tsp.**	**2 mL**
Salt	**1 tsp.**	**5 mL**
Celery salt	**½ tsp.**	**2 mL**
Bulgur	**⅓ cup**	**75 mL**

Combine all 9 ingredients in bowl. Mix well. Turn into greased 1 quart (1 L) casserole. Bake, uncovered, in 350°F (175°C) oven for 45 to 50 minutes until set. Serves 6.

1 serving contains: *219 Calories (916 kJ); 10.9 g Fat; 11 g Protein; 7 g Fiber*

Paré Pointer

Evil Knievel liked to take his pet cat along with him so he could make his jumps by a whisker.

SAUCY PATTIES

Patties have a meat texture. Cooked in a red sauce, this is a good company dish.

Large eggs	**4**	**4**
Dry bread crumbs	**2 cups**	**500 mL**
Chopped onion	**1 cup**	**250 mL**
Ground pecans (or walnuts)	**1 cup**	**250 mL**
Grated potato	**1 cup**	**250 mL**
Rolled oats (not instant)	**1 cup**	**250 mL**
Grated mozzarella cheese	**1 cup**	**250 mL**
Milk	**½ cup**	**125 mL**
Ketchup	**2 tbsp.**	**30 mL**
Gravy browner	**1 tsp.**	**5 mL**
Salt	**1½ tsp.**	**7 mL**
Pepper	**¼ tsp.**	**1 mL**
Cooking oil	**1 tbsp.**	**15 mL**
TOMATO ONION SAUCE		
Cooking oil	**1 tbsp.**	**15 mL**
Chopped onion	**2 cups**	**500 mL**
All-purpose flour	**2 tbsp.**	**30 mL**
Granulated sugar	**½ tsp.**	**2 mL**
Salt	**½ tsp.**	**2 mL**
Pepper	**¼ tsp.**	**1 mL**
Sweet basil	**¼ tsp.**	**1 mL**
Worcestershire sauce	**¼ tsp.**	**1 mL**
Tomato juice	**19 oz.**	**540 mL**

Beat eggs in bowl. Add next 11 ingredients. Mix. Let stand 10 minutes. Using ¼ cup (60 mL), shape into patties. Makes 16 patties.

Heat cooking oil in frying pan. Brown patties on both sides. Arrange in ungreased 3 quart (3 L) casserole.

Tomato Onion Sauce: Heat cooking oil in frying pan. Add onion. Sauté slowly until soft.

Mix in flour, sugar, salt, pepper and basil. Stir in Worcestershire sauce and tomato juice until mixture boils and thickens. Pour over patties. Cover. Bake in 350°F (175°C) oven for about 30 minutes. Serves 6.

***1 serving contains:** 562 Calories (2353 kJ); 27.1 g Fat; 20 g Protein; 6 g Fiber*

CHEESY PASTA CASSEROLE

With vegetables and dark leafy lettuce, this is a great meal.

Butter or hard margarine	**2 tbsp.**	**30 mL**
Sliced small zucchini, with peel	**4 cups**	**1 L**
Sliced fresh mushrooms	**1 cup**	**250 mL**
Salt, sprinkle		
Pepper, sprinkle		
Medium tomatoes, chopped	**4**	**4**
Torn romaine lettuce, lightly packed (or spinach)	**3 cups**	**750 mL**
Penne (or other pasta)	**8 oz.**	**250 g**
Boiling water	**3 qts.**	**3 L**
Cooking oil (optional)	**1 tbsp.**	**15 mL**
Salt	**2 tsp.**	**10 mL**
Grated mozzarella cheese (or 4 thick, packaged slices)	**1 cup**	**250 mL**
Grated medium or sharp Cheddar cheese (or 4 thick, packaged slices)	**1 cup**	**250 mL**

Melt butter in frying pan. Add zucchini and mushrooms. Sauté until soft and moisture has evaporated. Sprinkle with salt and pepper.

Add tomato and romaine lettuce. Stir. Simmer for 15 minutes, stirring often.

Cook penne in boiling water, cooking oil and salt in large uncovered pot for 11 to 13 minutes until tender but firm. Drain. Return penne to pot. Add zucchini mixture. Stir. Turn into ungreased 3 quart (3 L) casserole.

Cover with mozzarella cheese, followed by Cheddar cheese. Bake, uncovered, in 350°F (175°C) oven for about 30 minutes until hot and cheese is melted. Serves 6.

***1 serving contains:** 368 Calories (1541 kJ); 16.5 g Fat; 17 g Protein; 4 g Fiber*

COTTAGE CHEESE SQUARES

Attractive golden brown topping. Mild flavor.

Butter or hard margarine	**½ cup**	**125 mL**
Chopped onion	**1¼ cups**	**300 mL**
Creamed cottage cheese	**4 cups**	**1 L**
Rolled oats (not instant)	**1 cup**	**250 mL**
Crisp rice cereal	**6 cups**	**1.5 L**
Milk	**⅓ cup**	**75 mL**
Large eggs	**5**	**5**
Garlic powder	**¼ tsp.**	**1 mL**
Salt	**1 tsp.**	**5 mL**
Pepper	**¼ tsp.**	**1 mL**

Melt butter in frying pan. Add onion. Sauté until soft. Turn into large bowl.

Add remaining 8 ingredients. Mix well. Spread in greased 9 × 13 inch (22 × 33 cm) pan. Bake, uncovered, in 350°F (175°C) oven for 50 to 60 minutes. Let stand 10 minutes before serving. Cuts into 12 pieces.

1 piece contains: *288 Calories (1205 kJ); 14.8 g Fat; 16 g Protein; 1 g Fiber*

1. Corn Chip Salad, page 116
2. Spanish Lentil Pilaf, page 141
3. Fantasy Meatballs, page 84
4. Rice Chops, page 88
5. Vegetable Cutlets, page 50
6. Mushroom Sauce, page 132

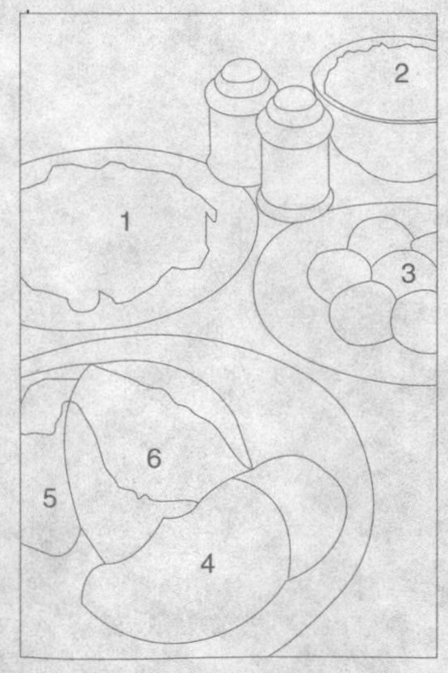

Tile Courtesy Of: Tile Town

Throw and Dinnerware Courtesy Of: Chintz & Company

Flatware Courtesy Of: IKEA

Napkin Courtesy Of: La Cache

RICE VEGGIE CASSEROLE

One of the most colorful dishes you can make.

Medium onion, chopped	**1**	**1**
Sliced celery	**1 cup**	**250 mL**
Canned tomatoes, drained, chopped, drained again	**19 oz.**	**540 mL**
Chili powder	**2 tsp.**	**10 mL**
Green pepper, seeded and chopped	**1**	**1**
Canned kidney beans, drained	**14 oz.**	**398 mL**
Cooked brown rice (about 1/4 cup, 60 mL, uncooked)	**1 cup**	**250 mL**
Canned kernel corn, drained	**12 oz.**	**341 mL**
Salt	**1/4 tsp.**	**1 mL**
Pepper	**1/8 tsp.**	**0.5 mL**
Crumbled whole wheat crackers (or unsalted corn chips)	**1/2 cup**	**125 mL**
Grated Edam cheese	**1/2 cup**	**125 mL**

Combine first 4 ingredients in saucepan. Heat to a simmer. Cover and simmer for 5 minutes. Stir once or twice during cooking. Remove from heat.

Add next 6 ingredients. Stir. Pour into ungreased 2 quart (2 L) casserole. Cover. Bake in 350°F (175°C) oven for 15 minutes.

Sprinkle with crackers and cheese. Bake, uncovered, for another 15 minutes. Serves 6 people, 1 cup (250 mL) each.

1 serving contains: *222 Calories (931 kJ); 4.6 g Fat; 10 g Protein; 8 g Fiber*

Pictured on page 53.

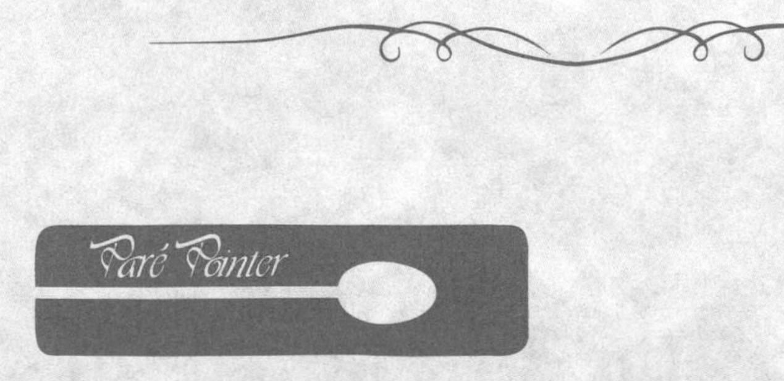

Would you have to go to Korea for Seoul food?

TOFU SAUSAGES

Good flavor. Rounds out a meal. Serve with ketchup.

Firm tofu	**1 lb.**	**454 g**
Cider vinegar	**1½ tbsp.**	**25 mL**
Chili powder	**2 tsp.**	**10 mL**
Salt	**1 tsp.**	**5 mL**
Pepper	**¼ tsp.**	**1 mL**
Whole oregano	**¾ tsp.**	**4 mL**
Paprika	**½ tsp.**	**2 mL**
Ground walnuts	**½ cup**	**125 mL**
Ground cumin	**¼ tsp.**	**1 mL**
Garlic powder	**¼ tsp.**	**1 mL**
Onion powder	**¼ tsp.**	**1 mL**
Bulgur	**½ cup**	**125 mL**
Rolled oats (not instant)	**1 cup**	**250 mL**
Cooking oil	**1 tbsp.**	**15 mL**

Mash tofu in medium bowl. Add next 10 ingredients. Mix.

Add bulgur and rolled oats. Stir. Let stand at least 10 minutes to absorb. Shape into sausages using about 2 tbsp. (30 mL) for each.

Heat cooking oil in frying pan. Brown sausages on all sides. Makes about 28.

1 sausage contains: *59 Calories (247 kJ); 3 g Fat; 4 g Protein; 1 g Fiber*

Pictured on page 53 and page 89.

BEAN SOUFFLÉ

A light delicate texture to this mildly spiced dish.

Egg yolks (large)	**4**	**4**
Ketchup	**2 tbsp.**	**30 mL**
Canned kidney beans, drained	**14 oz.**	**398 mL**
Salt	**½ tsp.**	**2 mL**
Pepper	**⅛ tsp.**	**0.5 mL**
Onion powder	**¼ tsp.**	**1 mL**
Grated medium or sharp Cheddar cheese	**1 cup**	**250 mL**
Egg whites (large), room temperature	**4**	**4**

(continued on next page)

Place first 6 ingredients in blender. Process until smooth. Pour into large bowl.

Add cheese. Stir.

Beat egg whites in medium bowl until stiff. Fold into bean mixture. Turn into greased 2 quart (2 L) casserole. Bake, uncovered, in 350°F (175°C) oven for 35 to 40 minutes until set. Serves 8.

1 serving contains: *146 Calories (610 kJ); 7.6 g Fat; 10 g Protein; 3 g Fiber*

VEGGIE WRAPS

While planned vegetables are good for these wraps, vegetables on hand can easily be substituted.

Flour tortillas, 7 or 9 inch (18 or 22 cm)	**4**	**4**
Plain yogurt	**¼ cup**	**60 mL**
Toasted sesame seeds	**2 tsp.**	**10 mL**
Cooked brown rice	**¼ cup**	**60 mL**
Chopped fresh broccoli, cooked tender-crisp (or raw)	**½ cup**	**125 mL**
Long narrow carrot strips, cooked tender-crisp (or raw)	**12**	**12**
Sprouts, bean, alfalfa or other	**¼ cup**	**60 mL**
Peanut Sauce, page 131, or Tahini Sauce, page 130	**4-6 tsp.**	**20-30 mL**

Stack the 4 tortillas between damp paper towels in microwave. Heat on high 40 to 55 seconds until warm, soft and pliable or wrap tortillas in foil to heat in 350°F (175°C) oven for about 8 minutes until warm. Arrange on working surface.

Divide next 6 ingredients down centers of tortillas.

Drizzle with Peanut Sauce, page 131, or Tahini Sauce, page 130. Roll up, folding in 1 side as you go. Makes 4.

1 wrap contains: *176 Calories (737 kJ); 3.4 g Fat; 7 g Protein; 2 g Fiber*

WHITE BEAN SAUSAGES

These fit right in to complete a meal. Excellent flavor.

Canned white kidney beans, drained	**19 oz.**	**540 mL**
Large egg	**1**	**1**
Ground sage	**½ tsp.**	**2 mL**
Salt	**½ tsp.**	**2 mL**
Pepper	**⅛ tsp.**	**0.5 mL**
Dry bread crumbs	**1 cup**	**250 mL**
Milk	**1 tbsp.**	**15 mL**
Cooking oil	**1 tbsp.**	**15 mL**

Mash beans on large plate with fork.

Beat egg in bowl. Mix in sage, salt and pepper. Add bread crumbs. Stir. Add beans. Mix well. Add a bit of milk if needed, just so mixture can be shaped. Shape into sausage rolls using about 2 tbsp. (30 mL) for each.

Heat cooking oil in frying pan. Brown sausages well on all sides. Add more cooking oil as needed. Makes 18.

***1 sausage contains:** 69 Calories (288 kJ); 1.5 g Fat; 3 g Protein; 1 g Fiber*

Pictured on page 89.

COULD-BE CHICKEN LOAF

Looks like a chicken loaf and could fool your guests.

Large eggs	**4**	**4**
Milk	**2 cups**	**500 mL**
Ground sage	**1 tsp.**	**5 mL**
Salt	**2 tsp.**	**10 mL**
Dry bread crumbs	**2 cups**	**500 mL**
Chopped walnuts (or other)	**2 cups**	**500 mL**

Beat eggs in bowl until frothy. Beat in milk, sage and salt.

Add bread crumbs and walnuts. Stir. Turn into greased 9 x 5 x 3 inch (22 x 12 x 7 cm) loaf pan. Bake, uncovered, in 350°F (175°C) oven for 40 to 45 minutes. Cuts into 10 slices.

***1 slice contains:** 315 Calories (1319 kJ); 20.4 g Fat; 11 g Protein; 2 g Fiber*

Exc.

CHICK PEA PATTIES

Lightly flavored with Parmesan cheese. More may be added if desired.

Bulgur	**½ cup**	**125 mL**
Boiling water	**½ cup**	**125 mL**
Large eggs	**2**	**2**
Canned chick peas (garbanzo beans), drained	**19 oz.**	**540 mL**
Dry bread crumbs	**¼ cup**	**60 mL**
Chopped fresh parsley (or 2 tsp., 10 mL, flakes)	**3 tbsp.**	**50 mL**
Grated Parmesan cheese	**2 tbsp.**	**30 mL**
Worcestershire sauce	**1 tsp.**	**5 mL**
Dry mustard powder	**½ tsp.**	**2 mL**
Salt	**½ tsp.**	**2 mL**
Whole oregano	**¼ tsp.**	**1 mL**
Dried sweet basil	**¼ tsp.**	**1 mL**
Garlic powder	**¼ tsp.**	**1 mL**
Pepper	**⅛ tsp.**	**0.5 mL**

Stir bulgur into boiling water in medium bowl. Cover. Let stand for 15 minutes.

Process eggs and chick peas in blender until smooth. Pour into bulgur. Stir.

Add remaining ingredients. Stir well. Shape into patties using ¼ cup (60 mL) for each. Fry in greased frying pan, browning both sides. Makes 10.

1 patty contains: *120 Calories (500 kJ); 2.6 g Fat; 6 g Protein; 3 g Fiber*

Pictured on page 107.

Paré Pointer

You need a canary and a potato to end up with potato chirps.

LEGUME PATTIES

Serve these with fried onions and all the trimmings.

Split peas (any color)	**1¼ cups**	**300 mL**
Boiling water	**3 cups**	**750 mL**
Large egg	**1**	**1**
Lemon juice, fresh or bottled	**1 tbsp.**	**15 mL**
Chopped onion	**½ cup**	**125 mL**
Ground thyme	**½ tsp.**	**2 mL**
Parsley flakes	**1½ tsp.**	**7 mL**
Soy sauce	**½ tsp.**	**2 mL**
Gravy browner	**1 tsp.**	**5 mL**
Salt	**1 tsp.**	**5 mL**
Pepper	**¼ tsp.**	**1 mL**
Cooked brown rice	**1 cup**	**250 mL**
All-purpose flour	**¼ cup**	**60 mL**
Dry bread crumbs	**1½ cups**	**375 mL**
All-purpose flour	**¼ cup**	**60 mL**

Cook peas in water for about 30 minutes until tender. Drain.

Put next 10 ingredients into blender. Process just to mix. Add peas. Process until smooth. Pour into bowl.

Stir in first amount of flour and bread crumbs. Let stand 10 minutes. Shape into patties using about ¼ cup (60 mL) for each.

Dip each patty in second amount of flour. Fry, browning both sides, in greased frying pan. Serve with your favorite barbecue sauce. Makes 18 patties.

1 patty contains: *123 Calories (513 kJ); 1.1 g Fat; 6 g Protein; 3 g Fiber*

Pictured on page 107.

Bakers usually go on strike because they want more dough.

SANDWICHED NUT LOAF

Nutty loaf leftovers can be used in a cold plate or in sandwiches.

Butter or hard margarine	**2 tbsp.**	**30 mL**
Chopped onion	**2 cups**	**500 mL**
Ground walnuts	**1½ cups**	**375 mL**
Ground pecans	**1½ cups**	**375 mL**
Rolled oats (not instant), run through blender	**1 cup**	**250 mL**
Coarsely crushed bran flakes cereal	**1 cup**	**250 mL**
Salt	**½ tsp.**	**2 mL**
Pepper	**⅛ tsp.**	**0.5 mL**
Whole oregano	**¼ tsp.**	**1 mL**
Garlic powder	**¼ tsp.**	**1 mL**
Ground thyme	**⅛ tsp.**	**0.5 mL**
Instant vegetable stock mix	**1 tbsp.**	**15 mL**
Boiling water	**¾ cup**	**175 mL**
Tomato slices, to cover	**6-8**	**6-8**
Grated medium Cheddar cheese	**¾ cup**	**175 mL**
Grated mozzarella cheese	**¾ cup**	**175 mL**

Melt butter in frying pan. Add onion. Sauté until soft. Turn into large bowl.

Add next 9 ingredients. Mix well.

Stir stock mix into boiling water in small bowl to dissolve. Pour over nut mixture. Stir. Pack ½ nut mixture in greased 8 x 4 x 3 inch (20 x 10 x 7 cm) loaf pan.

Layer tomato slices over top followed by both cheeses. Cover with second ½ nut mixture. Bake, uncovered, in 350°F (175°C) oven for about 30 to 35 minutes. Cuts into 10 slices.

1 slice contains: *331 Calories (1386 kJ); 25.2 g Fat; 11 g Protein; 4 g Fiber*

Pictured on page 35.

Paré Pointer

If you climb mountains over molehills, high blood pressure will surely develop.

CHILI

Colorful, chunky and very good and satisfying. Makes a family size or small party size quantity.

Cooking oil	**2 tbsp.**	**30 mL**
Chopped onion	**3 cups**	**750 mL**
Green pepper, chopped	**1**	**1**
Red pepper, chopped	**1**	**1**
Canned kidney beans, drained	**2 × 14 oz.**	**2 × 398 mL**
Canned pinto beans, drained	**14 oz.**	**398 mL**
Medium eggplant, peeled and diced	**1**	**1**
Canned stewed tomatoes	**14 oz.**	**398 mL**
Condensed tomato soup	**10 oz.**	**284 mL**
Cider vinegar	**1 tbsp.**	**15 mL**
Brown sugar, packed	**1/4 cup**	**60 mL**
Chili powder	**2 tbsp.**	**30 mL**
Canned sliced mushrooms, drained	**10 oz.**	**284 mL**
Garlic powder	**1/2 tsp.**	**2 mL**
Salt	**1 tsp.**	**5 mL**
Pepper	**1/4 tsp.**	**1 mL**

Heat cooking oil in frying pan. Add onion and peppers. Sauté until onion is soft. This may need to be done in two batches. Turn into large saucepan or Dutch oven.

Add remaining ingredients. Heat, stirring often until mixture starts to boil. Boil slowly, uncovered, for 5 to 10 minutes, stirring occasionally. Makes 10 1/4 cups (2.3 L), enough for 5 servings.

***1 serving contains:** 452 Calories (1891 kJ); 8.3 g Fat; 19 g Protein; 19 g Fiber*

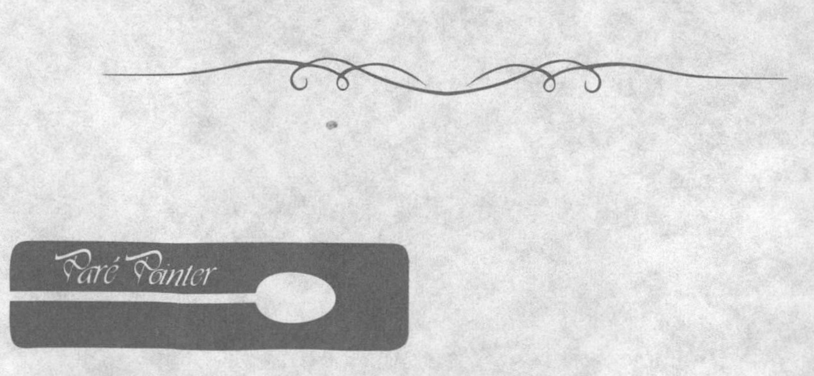

He had no worries about the rising cost of office supplies as long as it stayed stationery.

BEST ROAST

This would pass for a fabulous meat dish. If you are new to meatless cooking, make this your first try.

Large eggs	**2**	**2**
Soy sauce	**1 tbsp.**	**15 mL**
Medium firm tofu, drained and patted dry, cubed	**½ lb.**	**227 g**
Chopped walnuts	**½ cup**	**125 mL**
Cooking oil	**2 tbsp.**	**30 mL**
Chopped onion	**1½ cups**	**375 mL**
Chopped celery	**¾ cup**	**175 mL**
Sliced fresh mushrooms (or 10 oz., 284 mL can)	**2 cups**	**500 mL**
Envelope dry onion soup mix	**1 × 1½ oz.**	**1 × 42 g**
Whole oregano	**½ tsp.**	**2 mL**
Ground cumin	**½ tsp.**	**2 mL**
Dried sweet basil	**½ tsp.**	**2 mL**
Grated Parmesan cheese	**2 tbsp.**	**30 mL**
Dry bread crumbs	**1½ cups**	**375 mL**

Process eggs, soy sauce and tofu in blender until smooth.

Add walnuts. Process until walnuts are ground.

Heat cooking oil in frying pan. Add onion, celery and mushrooms. Sauté until soft. Turn into bowl.

Add blender ingredients. Add remaining 6 ingredients. Mix well. Pack into greased 8 × 4 × 3 inch (20 × 10 × 7 cm) loaf pan. Bake in 350°F (175°C) oven for about 45 minutes. Let stand for 10 minutes. Turn out onto serving platter. Cuts into 10 slices.

1 slice contains: *217 Calories (909 kJ); 11.2 g Fat; 10 g Protein; 1 g Fiber*

Pictured on page 35.

Paré Pointer

They didn't pay for their clothes. It was on the cuff.

FAVORITE ROAST

When you serve this, your guests will think they are eating meat. Use leftovers for sandwiches or a picnic.

Large eggs	**3**	**3**
Creamed cottage cheese	**2 cups**	**500 mL**
Milk	**1/4 cup**	**60 mL**
Liquid gravy browner	**1/2 tsp.**	**2 mL**
Finely chopped onion	**1 cup**	**250 mL**
Instant vegetable stock mix	**1 tbsp.**	**15 mL**
Cooking oil	**1/4 cup**	**60 mL**
Ground pecans	**1/2 cup**	**125 mL**
Bran flakes cereal	**4 1/2 cups**	**1.1 L**
Grated sharp Cheddar cheese	**1/3 cup**	**75 mL**
Ground thyme	**1/4 tsp.**	**1 mL**
Ketchup	**2 tbsp.**	**30 mL**

Beat eggs in bowl until blended. Add cottage cheese, milk and gravy browner. Beat to mix.

Add next 7 ingredients. Mix well. Pack in greased 9 x 5 x 3 inch (22 x 12 x 7 cm) loaf pan.

Spread ketchup over top. Bake, uncovered, in 375°F (190°C) oven for 45 minutes. Serve hot. Cuts into 10 slices.

1 slice contains: *279 Calories (1166 kJ); 15.2 g Fat; 13 g Protein; 4 g Fiber*

Was today really necessary?

LENTIL STEW

This good stove top stew is thick with vegetables.

Water	**6 cups**	**1.5 L**
Instant vegetable stock mix	**2 tbsp.**	**30 mL**
Tomato paste	**5½ oz.**	**156 mL**
Brown rice	**¼ cup**	**60 mL**
Bite size cut carrots	**2 cups**	**500 mL**
Bite size cut potatoes	**2 cups**	**500 mL**
Sliced celery	**1 cup**	**250 mL**
Chopped onion	**1½ cups**	**375 mL**
Red lentils	**1 cup**	**250 mL**
Bite size cut yellow turnip	**1 cup**	**250 mL**
Salt	**¾ tsp.**	**4 mL**
Pepper	**¼ tsp.**	**1 mL**
Garlic powder	**¼ tsp.**	**1 mL**
Granulated sugar	**½ tsp.**	**2 mL**
Bay leaf	**1**	**1**
Peas, fresh or frozen	**1 cup**	**250 mL**

Place all ingredients, except peas, in large stock pot or Dutch oven. Stir often until mixture boils. Boil gently, covered, for 1¾ hours. Stir occasionally to prevent sticking.

Add peas. Boil until peas are cooked. Discard bay leaf. Makes 10¾ cups (2.7 L), enough for 5 servings.

Note: This can be simmered for 1½ hours, then cooled and refrigerated. Reheat for ½ hour the day of serving.

1 serving contains: *360 Calories (1505 kJ); 2.9 g Fat; 18 g Protein; 13 g Fiber*

Pictured on page 89.

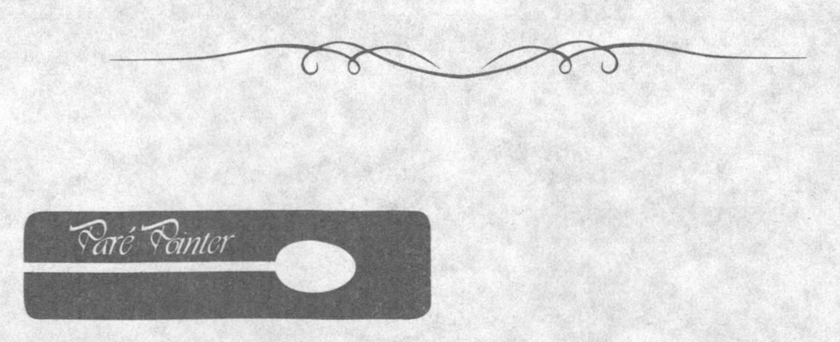

Little Susie asked if hail was hard-boiled rain.

FANTASY MEATBALLS

The fantasy is that it's hard to tell it isn't meat.

Large eggs	**5**	**5**
Creamed cottage cheese	**1 cup**	**250 mL**
Dried sweet basil	**1 tsp.**	**5 mL**
Salt	**3/4 tsp.**	**4 mL**
Pepper	**1/8 tsp.**	**0.5 mL**
Chopped onion	**3/4 cup**	**175 mL**
Grated mozzarella cheese	**1 cup**	**250 mL**
Dry bread crumbs	**2 cups**	**500 mL**
Ground walnuts	**1 cup**	**250 mL**
Parsley flakes	**1 tsp.**	**5 mL**
Poultry seasoning	**1 1/4 tsp.**	**6 mL**
Tomato sauce	**7 1/2 oz.**	**213 mL**
Water	**1 cup**	**250 mL**
Granulated sugar	**1/2 tsp.**	**2 mL**

Beat eggs in mixing bowl until smooth. Add cottage cheese, basil, salt and pepper. Beat to mix.

Add next 6 ingredients. Stir. Let stand 10 minutes. Shape into 1 1/2 inch (4 cm) balls. Arrange in ungreased 9 x 13 inch (22 x 33 cm) pan in single layer.

Stir tomato sauce, water and sugar together in small bowl. Pour over balls. Bake, uncovered, in 350°F (175°C) oven for about 35 minutes. Makes about 3 dozen. Serves 8.

***1 serving contains:** 313 Calories (1310 kJ); 14.4 g Fat; 18 g Protein; 2 g Fiber*

Pictured on page 71.

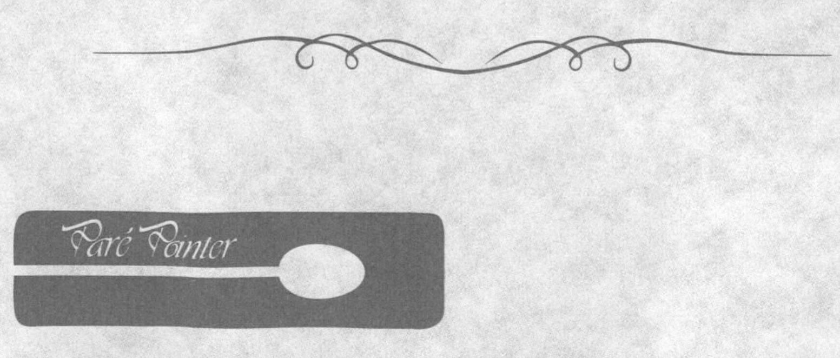

She's too religious for him. She worships money and he doesn't have any.

CHEESY NUT BAKE

This nutty dish has a brown crumb topping. Good flavor. Looks like a meatloaf.

Butter or hard margarine	**2 tbsp.**	**30 mL**
Finely chopped onion	**1⅓ cups**	**325 mL**
Water	**½ cup**	**125 mL**
Natural bran	**1½ cups**	**375 mL**
Grated sharp Cheddar cheese	**2 cups**	**500 mL**
Lemon juice, fresh or bottled	**2 tbsp.**	**30 mL**
Large eggs, fork-beaten	**3**	**3**
Ground walnuts	**1½ cups**	**375 mL**
Salt	**1 tsp.**	**5 mL**
Pepper	**¼ tsp.**	**1 mL**
TOPPING		
Butter or hard margarine	**1 tbsp.**	**15 mL**
Dry bread crumbs	**¼ cup**	**60 mL**

Melt butter in frying pan. Add onion. Sauté until clear and beginning to brown. Remove from heat.

Mix in next 8 ingredients in order given. Turn into greased 2 quart (2 L) casserole.

Topping: Melt butter in small saucepan. Stir in bread crumbs. Sprinkle over top. Bake, uncovered, in 350°F (175°C) oven for about 30 minutes until browned and heated through. Serve with Red Sauce, page 130. Serves 6.

1 serving contains: *468 Calories (1960 kJ); 36.4 g Fat; 22 g Protein; 9 g Fiber*

She thought lunatiks were little bugs that lived on the moon.

MOCK MEATBALLS

Great-looking casserole full of meatballs smothered in sauce.

Rolled oats (not instant)	**1 cup**	**250 mL**
Soda cracker crumbs	**1 cup**	**250 mL**
Salt	**1 tsp.**	**5 mL**
Pepper	**1 tsp.**	**5 mL**
Ground sage	**1/2 tsp.**	**2 mL**
Chili powder	**1/2 tsp.**	**2 mL**
Creamed cottage cheese	**1 cup**	**250 mL**
Finely chopped onion	**1 1/2 cups**	**375 mL**
Large eggs	**2**	**2**
Condensed cream of mushroom soup	**10 oz.**	**284 mL**
Water (or milk)	**1/3 cup**	**75 mL**

Measure first 6 ingredients into bowl. Stir.

Add cottage cheese, onion and eggs. Mix well. Let stand 10 minutes for crumbs and oatmeal to absorb moisture. Shape into 1 1/2 inch (4 cm) balls. Arrange in ungreased 9 x 9 inch (22 x 22 cm) casserole.

Stir soup and water together in bowl. Pour over balls. Cover. Bake in 350°F (175°C) oven for about 45 minutes. Remove cover. Bake for about 30 minutes more until browned slightly. Makes about 27 balls. Serves 6.

1 serving contains: *256 Calories (1071 kJ); 10.3 g Fat; 12 g Protein; 3 g Fiber*

MUSHROOM RICE PATTIES

These have a good chewy texture. Different.

Brown rice	**1 1/3 cups**	**325 mL**
Water	**2 2/3 cups**	**650 mL**
Cooking oil	**1 tbsp.**	**15 mL**
Finely chopped onion	**1/2 cup**	**125 mL**
Finely chopped mushrooms	**2 cups**	**500 mL**
Grated medium or sharp Cheddar cheese	**1/2 cup**	**125 mL**
Salt	**3/4 tsp.**	**4 mL**
Pepper	**1/4 tsp.**	**1 mL**
Garlic powder (optional)	**1/8 tsp.**	**0.5 mL**

(continued on next page)

Cook rice in water for about 45 minutes until tender and water is absorbed. Add a touch more water if needed.

Heat cooking oil in frying pan. Add onion and mushrooms. Sauté until soft and moisture has evaporated. Mix into rice.

Add remaining ingredients. Stir well. Shape into patties using about 1/4 cup (60 mL) for each. Fry in greased frying pan browning both sides. Makes 15 patties.

1 patty contains: *93 Calories (390 kJ); 2.8 g Fat; 3 g Protein; 1 g Fiber*

ZUCCHINI CUTLETS

So colorful with red and green showing throughout. A wonderful addition to a meal.

Grated carrot	**1/2 cup**	**125 mL**
Chopped onion	**1/2 cup**	**125 mL**
Chopped red pepper	**1/4 cup**	**60 mL**
Chopped green pepper	**1/4 cup**	**60 mL**
Fine soda cracker crumbs	**2 cups**	**500 mL**
All-purpose flour	**1/4 cup**	**60 mL**
Baking powder	**1 tsp.**	**5 mL**
Salt	**3/4 tsp.**	**4 mL**
Pepper	**1/8 tsp.**	**0.5 mL**
Grated zucchini, with peel	**3 cups**	**750 mL**
Large eggs, fork-beaten	**2**	**2**
Cooking oil	**2 tbsp.**	**30 mL**

Measure first 9 ingredients into large bowl. Stir.

Mix in zucchini and eggs. Shape into cutlets (patties) using about 1/4 cup (60 mL) for each.

Heat cooking oil in frying pan. Brown cutlets on both sides. Makes about 1 dozen.

1 cutlet contains: *117 Calories (489 kJ); 5.1 g Fat; 3 g Protein; 1 g Fiber*

Pictured on front cover.

RICE CHOPS

It's surprising that only a slight taste of peanut butter remains in these chops. Easy to double the recipe. Chewy texture.

Boiling water	**1 cup**	**250 mL**
Smooth peanut butter	**½ cup**	**125 mL**
Instant rice	**1 cup**	**250 mL**
Salt	**½ tsp.**	**2 mL**
Celery salt	**½ tsp.**	**2 mL**
Onion powder	**¼ tsp.**	**1 mL**
Large egg, fork-beaten	**1**	**1**

Measure first 6 ingredients into saucepan. Heat and stir until mixture comes to a boil. Remove from heat. Set saucepan in cold water in sink to hasten cooling. Stir often.

Stir egg into cooled mixture. Let stand for at least 30 minutes in refrigerator to firm up enough to handle. Using about ¼ cup (60 mL) each, shape into chops (patties). Arrange on greased baking sheet. Bake in 375°F (190°C) oven for 10 minutes. Turn chops. Continue to bake for 10 minutes more. Makes 6 small chops.

1 chop contains: *209 Calories (875 kJ); 12.2 g Fat; 8 g Protein; 2 g Fiber*

Pictured on page 71.

1. Lentil Stew, page 83
2. Pasta Veggie Salad, page 111
3. White Bean Sausages, page 76
4. Red Sauce, page 130
5. Tofu Sausages, page 74

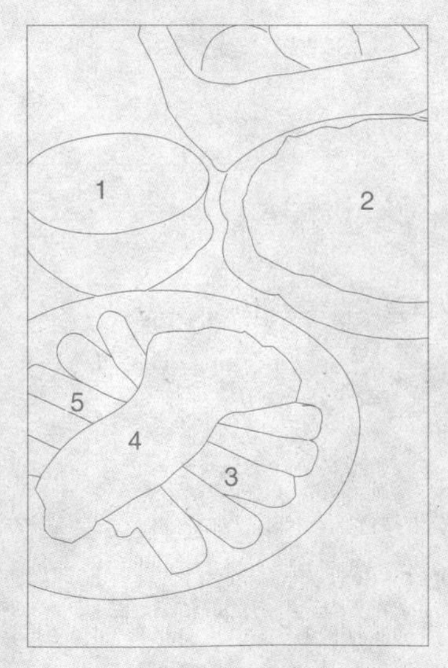

Pottery Courtesy Of: Clayworks Studios

Basket Courtesy Of: The Bay

Napkins Courtesy Of: La Cache

OATMEAL PATTIES

By using half of the mushroom soup, there is enough left for sauce to pour over the patties.

Butter or hard margarine	**1 tbsp.**	**15 mL**
Chopped onion	**1 cup**	**250 mL**
Large eggs	**2**	**2**
Rolled oats (not instant)	**1 cup**	**250 mL**
Condensed cream of mushroom soup (see Note)	**½ × 10 oz.**	**½ × 284 mL**
Worcestershire sauce	**½ tsp.**	**2 mL**
Salt	**½ tsp.**	**2 mL**
Garlic powder	**⅛ tsp.**	**0.5 mL**
Ground thyme	**⅛ tsp.**	**0.5 mL**
Cooking oil	**1 tbsp.**	**15 mL**

Melt butter in frying pan. Add onion. Sauté slowly until soft.

Beat eggs in bowl until frothy. Add next 6 ingredients. Add onion. Mix well. Let stand 10 minutes.

Heat cooking oil in frying pan. Drop mixture by ¼ cup (60 mL) into pan. Press with back of spoon to shape into a round patty. Brown both sides. Makes 6.

Note: Heat second half of mushroom soup, thinning with a bit of milk, to serve as sauce if desired.

1 patty contains: *158 Calories (661 kJ); 8.8 g Fat; 5 g Protein; 2 g Fiber*

OATMEAL BURGERS: Insert in hamburger buns. Load up with ketchup, relish, onion, tomato, cheese or whatever else you like.

Pictured on page 107.

If you forgot to put the "y" on lady would she become a young lad?

WIENERS AND BEANS

The yummiest ever! Serve as a main course or serve over toast for lunch. A tasty mild nip.

Canned beans in tomato sauce	**14 oz.**	**398 mL**
Package tofu wieners, cut in 1/2 inch (12 mm) pieces	**1/2 × 12 oz.**	**1/2 × 340 g**
Chopped onion	**1/2 cup**	**125 mL**
Canned beans in tomato sauce	**14 oz.**	**398 mL**
Package tofu wieners, cut in 1/2 inch (12 mm) pieces	**1/2 × 12 oz.**	**1/2 × 340 g**
Chopped onion	**1/2 cup**	**125 mL**
Condensed tomato soup	**10 oz.**	**284 mL**
Mild molasses	**3 tbsp.**	**50 mL**
Prepared mustard	**1 tbsp.**	**15 mL**
Salt	**1/2 tsp.**	**2 mL**
Pepper	**1/4 tsp.**	**1 mL**

Layer first 6 ingredients, in order given, in bean pot or Dutch oven.

Mix remaining 5 ingredients in bowl. Pour over top. Poke knife down into beans to allow sauce to penetrate. Cover. Bake in 350°F (175°C) oven for 1 1/2 hours. Remove cover. Bake for 30 minutes more. Makes 5 cups (1.25 L).

***1 cup (250 mL) contains:** 339 Calories (1417 kJ); 3.2 g Fat; 27 g Protein; 11 g Fiber*

POTLUCK BAKED BEANS

A bean dish to end all bean dishes. Different and excellent.

Canned baked beans in tomato sauce	**2 × 14 oz.**	**2 × 398 mL**
Canned kidney beans, with liquid	**14 oz.**	**398 mL**
Canned lima beans, drained	**14 oz.**	**398 mL**
Canned mushroom pieces, drained	**10 oz.**	**284 mL**
Cooking oil	**2 tbsp.**	**30 mL**
Chopped onion	**2 1/2 cups**	**625 mL**
Brown sugar, packed	**3/4 cup**	**175 mL**
White vinegar	**1/4 cup**	**60 mL**
Liquid smoke	**1 tsp.**	**5 mL**

(continued on next page)

Combine first 4 ingredients in large bowl.

Heat cooking oil in frying pan. Add onion. Sauté until soft and clear. Stir into bean mixture.

Add remaining ingredients. Stir well. Turn into ungreased 3 quart (3 L) casserole. Bake, uncovered, in 325°F (160°C) oven for 1 hour. Serves 10.

***1 serving contains:** 271 Calories (1134 kJ); 4.0 g Fat; 10 g Protein; 11 g Fiber*

CHEESY PATTIES

A great cheese and tomato flavor.

Condensed tomato soup	**1/3 cup**	**75 mL**
Large egg	**1**	**1**
Prepared mustard	**1 tsp.**	**5 mL**
Salt	**1/2 tsp.**	**2 mL**
Pepper	**1/4 tsp.**	**1 mL**
Bulgur	**1/4 cup**	**60 mL**
Boiling water	**1/4 cup**	**60 mL**
Dry bread crumbs (or 2 cups, 500 mL, fresh)	**1 1/2 cups**	**375 mL**
Grated medium or sharp Cheddar cheese	**2 cups**	**500 mL**
Soda cracker crumbs	**1/2 cup**	**125 mL**
Cooking oil	**2 tbsp.**	**30 mL**

Stir first 5 ingredients well in medium bowl.

Combine bulgur and boiling water in small bowl. Cover. Let stand 15 minutes. Add to soup mixture.

Stir in bread crumbs and cheese. Let stand 10 minutes. Shape into 10 patties. They are easier to shape if you moisten your hands with water.

Coat patties with cracker crumbs. Brown on both sides in hot cooking oil. Add more oil if necessary. Makes 12.

***1 patty contains:** 195 Calories (814 kJ); 10.6 g Fat; 8 g Protein; 1 g Fiber*

Pictured on page 107.

TOMATO ONION QUICHE

This serves as a main course or as an appetizer. Looks colorful with a red top.

Cooking oil	**1½ tbsp.**	**25 mL**
Chopped onion	**1½ cups**	**375 mL**
Whole Wheat Pastry pie shell, page 106, 9 inch (22 cm), unbaked	**1**	**1**
Grated medium or sharp Cheddar cheese	**1½ cups**	**375 mL**
Large eggs	**3**	**3**
All-purpose flour	**2 tbsp.**	**30 mL**
Dijon mustard	**1½ tsp.**	**7 mL**
Skim evaporated milk (or light cream)	**1 cup**	**250 mL**
Salt	**½ tsp.**	**2 mL**
Pepper	**⅛ tsp.**	**0.5 mL**
Medium tomatoes, sliced	**2**	**2**
TOPPING		
Parsley flakes	**½ tsp.**	**2 mL**
Dried sweet basil	**¼ tsp.**	**1 mL**
Salt	**⅛ tsp.**	**0.5 mL**
Pepper, sprinkle		
Onion powder, sprinkle		

Heat cooking oil in frying pan. Add onion. Sauté until soft. Cool.

Spread onion in bottom of pie shell. Spread cheese over onion.

Beat eggs, flour and mustard in bowl until smooth. Add milk, salt and pepper. Beat. Pour over cheese in pie shell.

Arrange tomato slices on top, overlapping a bit if necessary.

Topping: Mix parsley flakes, basil and salt. Sprinkle over tomato slices.

Sprinkle with pepper and onion powder. Bake on bottom rack in 350°F (175°C) oven for 35 to 40 minutes until a knife inserted near center comes out clean. Cuts into 6 wedges for main course (or 10 wedges for appetizer course).

1 main course wedge contains: *435 Calories (1818 kJ); 28.9 g Fat; 17 g Protein; 3 g Fiber*

Pictured on front cover.

QUESADILLAS

Bake these kay-sah-DEE-yahs in the oven. Everybody's favorite.

Cream cheese, softened	**4 oz.**	**125 g**
Salsa, medium	**1/3 cup**	**75 mL**
Chopped green pepper	**1/3 cup**	**75 mL**
Large tomato, seeded and diced	**1**	**1**
Canned chopped green chilies, drained	**4 oz.**	**114 mL**
Green onions, chopped	**3**	**3**
Flour tortillas (10 inch, 25 cm)	**6**	**6**
Grated Monterey Jack cheese (or medium Cheddar if preferred)	**1 1/2 cups**	**375 mL**
Guacamole, page 14, salsa and sour cream, for dipping		

Mash cream cheese and salsa together with fork in shallow bowl or plate. Set aside.

Toss next 4 ingredients in small bowl.

Lay tortillas on working surface. Spread 1/2 of each tortilla with cream cheese mixture to 1/2 inch (12 mm) from edge. Sprinkle green pepper mixture over cream cheese mixture.

Sprinkle each with grated cheese. Fold uncovered half over filling. Press edges lightly with your hand. Arrange on ungreased baking sheet. Bake in 425°F (220°C) oven for 10 to 15 minutes or toast under broiler.

Cut into 4 wedges each. Serve with dipping sauces. Makes 24 wedges.

***1 wedge contains:** 94 Calories (393 kJ); 4.3 g Fat; 4 g Protein; trace Fiber*

QUESADILLA APPETIZERS: Use about 10 flour tortillas, 8 inch (20 cm) size. Follow above recipe. Cut each into 6 wedges for a more manageable size. Makes 60 wedges.

"MEAT" SCRAMBLE PIE

Don't be intimidated by the long list of ingredients. They go together quickly and easily. A very versatile mixture.

"MEAT" SCRAMBLE		
Grated onion	1 cup	250 mL
Grated carrot	½ cup	125 mL
Bulgur	½ cup	125 mL
Yellow split peas	⅔ cup	150 mL
Water	3 cups	700 mL
Ketchup	2 tbsp.	30 mL
Salt	1 tsp.	5 mL
Pepper	¼ tsp.	1 mL
Parsley flakes	1 tsp.	5 mL
Yeast extract (such as Marmite or Vegemite)	1 tsp.	5 mL
Garlic powder	½ tsp.	2 mL
Whole oregano	½ tsp.	2 mL
Ground cumin	¼ tsp.	1 mL
Dry mustard powder	⅛ tsp.	0.5 mL
Rolled oats (not instant)	1¼ cups	275 mL
Dry bread crumbs, if needed for thickening		
Whole Wheat Pastry, page 106, enough for 2 crust, 9 inch (22 cm) pie		

"Meat" Scramble: Combine first 5 ingredients in heavy saucepan. Cover and simmer for about 45 minutes, stirring often, until vegetables are cooked. Stir more often towards the last as it tends to stick.

Stir in next 10 ingredients in order given. Stir well. Remove from heat. Cool.

If mixture is very moist, add ¼ cup (60 mL) bread crumbs. Stir. Let stand 10 minutes to absorb. Add more crumbs if needed. Makes 4 cups (1 L).

Roll out bottom pastry crust on lightly floured surface. Line pie plate. Fill with cooled mixture. Roll out top crust. Dampen edge of bottom crust. Cover with top crust. Crimp and seal. Cut slits in top. Bake on bottom shelf in 400°F (205°C) oven for 25 to 30 minutes until browned. Cuts into 6 thick wedges.

1 wedge contains: *389 Calories (1626 kJ); 14 g Fat; 13 g Protein; 9 g Fiber*

(continued on next page)

SCRAMBLE TURNOVERS: Use "Meat" Scramble, page 96, as filling for pastry rounds for appetizers. Dampen edges. Fold over. Crimp edge. Cut 2 or 3 tiny slits in top. Bake as above until browned.

SCRAMBLE PATTIES: Add enough bread crumbs to "Meat" Scramble, page 96, so mixture can be handled. Shape into patties using ¼ cup (60 mL) each. Brown both sides in frying pan. Makes about 16.

QUICHE LORNE

Not quite Lorraine with veggie bacon but it is just as good.

Butter or hard margarine	**1 tbsp.**	**15 mL**
Green onions, thinly sliced	**6**	**6**
Veggie back bacon slices, chopped	**6**	**6**
Grated cheese, mixture of Swiss and medium or sharp Cheddar	**1½ cups**	**375 mL**
Whole Wheat Pastry pie shell, page 106, 9 inch (22 cm), unbaked	**1**	**1**
Large eggs	**3**	**3**
Skim evaporated milk	**13½ oz.**	**385 mL**
Salt	**½ tsp.**	**2 mL**
Pepper	**¼ tsp.**	**1 mL**
Ground nutmeg	**⅛ tsp.**	**0.5 mL**

Melt butter in small frying pan. Add onion. Sauté until soft. Cool.

Spread bacon and cheeses in pie shell. Sprinkle onion over top.

Beat eggs in small bowl. Add milk, salt, pepper and nutmeg. Beat to mix. Pour over mixture into pie shell. Bake in 350°F (175°C) oven for about 45 minutes until a knife inserted near center comes out clean. Cuts into 6 wedges for main course (or 10 wedges for appetizer).

1 main course wedge contains: *422 Calories (1760 kJ); 25.8 g Fat; 24 g Protein; 2 g Fiber*

OATMEAL PIE SHELL

Makes a good tasting base for a chilled pie. Try with Butterscotch Pie, page 105.

Butter or hard margarine	**⅓ cup**	**75 mL**
Rolled oats, ground in blender (measure after grinding)	**1¼ cups**	**300 mL**
Brown sugar, packed	**¼ cup**	**60 mL**
Ground cinnamon (optional)	**¼ tsp.**	**1 mL**

Melt butter in saucepan.

Stir in remaining ingredients. Press in 9 inch (22 cm) pie plate. Bake in 375°F (190°C) oven for about 10 minutes. Makes 1 pie shell.

1 pie shell contains: *1202 Calories (5031 kJ); 71.3 g Fat; 18 g Protein; 10 g Fiber*

VEGETABLE PIZZA

Different from the usual pizza to be sure. Mild flavor with a good vegetable mixture.

CRUST		
Biscuit mix	**2 cups**	**500 mL**
Milk	**½ cup**	**125 mL**
FILLING		
Tomato sauce	**7½ oz.**	**213 mL**
Whole oregano	**½ tsp.**	**2 mL**
Dried sweet basil	**½ tsp.**	**2 mL**
Garlic powder	**⅛ tsp.**	**0.5 mL**
Granulated sugar	**½ tsp.**	**2 mL**
Finely chopped onion	**¾ cup**	**175 mL**
Broccoli florets	**2 cups**	**500 mL**
Sliced fresh mushrooms	**1 cup**	**250 mL**
Boiling water		
Grated mozzarella cheese	**1 cup**	**250 mL**
Canned whole baby corn, drained, halved	**8**	**8**
Grated mozzarella cheese	**2 cups**	**500 mL**

(continued on next page)

Crust: Stir biscuit mix with milk to form a ball. Knead on lightly floured surface 6 to 8 times. Spread on greased 12 inch (30 cm) pizza pan.

Filling: Stir first 5 ingredients together. Spread over pizza crust.

Cook onion, broccoli and mushrooms in boiling water until tender-crisp. Drain.

Sprinkle first amount of mozzarella cheese over sauce. Spoon cooked vegetables over top, then add corn. Sprinkle with remaining cheese. Bake on bottom rack in 425°F (220°C) oven for 12 to 15 minutes. Cuts into 8 wedges.

1 wedge contains: *339 Calories (1419 kJ); 13.3 g Fat; 17 g Protein; 2 g Fiber*

Pictured on page 125.

DEEP FRUIT PIE

A handy from-the-shelf pie. Serve hot with ice cream or cold with whipped cream.

Canned peaches, pears or other fruit, drained and juice reserved, cubed	**2 × 14 oz.**	**2 × 398 mL**
Granulated sugar	**2/3 cup**	**150 mL**
All-purpose flour	**3 tbsp.**	**50 mL**
Lemon juice, fresh or bottled	**1 tsp.**	**5 mL**
Reserved fruit juice	**1/2 cup**	**125 mL**
Whole Wheat Pastry, page 106, enough for 1 crust, 9 inch (22 cm) pie		
Granulated sugar	**1/2 tsp.**	**2 mL**

Spread fruit in bottom of ungreased 1½ quart (1.5 L) casserole.

Mix first amount of sugar and flour in saucepan. Add lemon juice and fruit juice gradually, stirring until no lumps remain. Heat and stir until mixture boils and thickens. Cool. Pour over fruit.

Roll out pastry on lightly floured surface. Cut 1 inch (2.5 cm) larger than needed to cover fruit. Lay pastry over fruit. Press edges up slightly around inside of dish. Cut slits in top.

Sprinkle with remaining sugar. Bake, uncovered, in 400°F (205°C) oven for about 30 minutes until browned. Serves 6.

1 serving contains: *340 Calories (1421 kJ); 12.3 g Fat; 3 g Protein; 3 g Fiber*

PIZZA

The vegetables are well seasoned. The flavor of a red pepper adds to the taste.

PIZZA CRUST		
All-purpose flour	1½ cups	375 mL
Baking powder	2 tsp.	10 mL
Envelope instant yeast	1 × ¼ oz.	1 × 8 g
Cooking oil	2 tbsp.	30 mL
Warm water	⅔ cup	150 mL
FILLING		
Cooking oil	1 tbsp.	15 mL
Chopped onion	1¼ cups	300 mL
Garlic clove, minced (or ¼ tsp., 1 mL, garlic powder)	1	1
Grated zucchini, with peel	2 cups	500 mL
Medium tomatoes, chopped	3	3
Ketchup	2 tbsp.	30 mL
Dried sweet basil	½ tsp.	2 mL
Whole oregano	½ tsp.	2 mL
Granulated sugar	½ tsp.	2 mL
Salt	½ tsp.	2 mL
Pepper	⅛ tsp.	0.5 mL
TOPPING		
Small fresh mushrooms, sliced	6-10	6-10
Red or green pepper strips	½ cup	125 mL
Medium tomato, diced	1	1
Veggie pepperoni slices, quartered	5-7	5-7
Grated mozzarella cheese	2 cups	500 mL

Pizza Crust: Stir flour, baking powder and yeast together in bowl.

Add cooking oil and warm water. Mix. Knead on lightly floured surface 25 to 30 times until smooth and elastic. Spray 12 inch (30 cm) pizza pan with non-stick cooking spray. Roll and stretch dough to fit pan.

Filling: Heat cooking oil in frying pan. Add onion and garlic. Sauté until soft.

Add next 8 ingredients. Sauté until sauce is thickened. Cool. Spread over pizza crust.

(continued on next page)

Topping: Scatter mushrooms, red pepper, tomato and pepperoni slices over top. Cover with cheese. Bake on bottom rack in 425°F (220°C) oven for 12 to 15 minutes. Cuts into 8 wedges.

1 wedge contains: *278 Calories (1163 kJ); 10.8 g Fat; 15 g Protein; 3 g Fiber*

ZUCCHINI QUICHE

A creamy white custard base with bits of cheese showing.

Cooking oil	**2 tbsp.**	**30 mL**
Thinly sliced zucchini, with peel	**1½ cups**	**375 mL**
Chopped onion	**½ cup**	**125 mL**
Garlic powder (or ½ garlic clove, minced)	**⅛ tsp.**	**0.5 mL**
Grated medium or sharp Cheddar cheese	**1½ cups**	**375 mL**
Whole Wheat Pastry pie shell, page 106, 9 inch (22 cm), unbaked	**1**	**1**
Large eggs	**4**	**4**
Milk	**1⅓ cups**	**325 mL**
Salt	**½ tsp.**	**2 mL**
Pepper	**¼ tsp.**	**1 mL**

Heat cooking oil in frying pan. Add zucchini, onion and garlic powder. Sauté until soft. Remove from heat. Cool.

Spread cheese in bottom of pie shell. Spoon cooled zucchini mixture over top.

Beat eggs in medium bowl until smooth. Add milk, salt and pepper. Mix. Pour over zucchini mixture. Bake on bottom shelf in 350°F (175°C) oven for about 1 hour until set. Cuts into 6 wedges for a main dish serving (or into 10 wedges for an appetizer serving).

1 large wedge contains: *421 Calories (1762 kJ); 31.2 g Fat; 16 g Protein; 2 g Fiber*

VEGGIE PASTIES

These exceptionally good pasties can be eaten hot or cold, can be carried in a lunch bag, or can be eaten as a snack.

Cooking oil	**1 tbsp.**	**15 mL**
Chopped onion	**½ cup**	**125 mL**
Diced carrot	**½ cup**	**125 mL**
Diced potato	**½ cup**	**125 mL**
Diced yellow turnip	**½ cup**	**125 mL**
Water	**2 tbsp.**	**30 mL**
Peas, fresh or frozen	**⅓ cup**	**75 mL**
Salt	**½ tsp.**	**2 mL**
Pepper	**⅛ tsp.**	**0.5 mL**
Whole oregano	**⅛ tsp.**	**0.5 mL**
Ground thyme	**⅛ tsp.**	**0.5 mL**
Grated medium or sharp Cheddar cheese	**1½ cups**	**375 mL**
Whole Wheat Pastry, page 106, enough for 3 crusts, 9 inch (22 cm) each		

Heat cooking oil in saucepan. Add onion, carrot, potato, turnip and water. Cover. Simmer until vegetables are almost cooked. Remove from heat.

Add peas, salt, pepper, oregano and thyme. Stir.

Mix in cheese. Remove from heat. Cool.

Roll pastry on lightly floured surface. Cut out saucer size rounds. Divide vegetable mixture among centers of pastry using about 2 tbsp. (30 mL) for each. Dampen edges of each half circle. Fold over. Crimp to seal. Cut 3 slits in tops of each. Arrange on ungreased baking sheets. Bake in 375°F (190°C) oven for 25 to 30 minutes until lightly browned. Makes 12.

1 pasty contains: *345 Calories (1442 kJ); 24.6 g Fat; 8 g Protein; 3 g Fiber*

SAUSAGE PASTIES: If you have Tofu Sausages, page 74, or White Bean Sausages, page 76, in your freezer, chop 2 of them and add to vegetables.

WIENER PASTIES: Chop 2 tofu wieners and add to vegetables.

TAMALE PIE

A bright yellow topping over a dark reddish filling.

Cooking oil	**1 tbsp.**	**15 mL**
Chopped onion	**1 cup**	**250 mL**
Chopped green pepper	**½ cup**	**125 mL**
Garlic clove, minced (or ¼ tsp., 1 mL, garlic powder)	**1**	**1**
Canned tomatoes, with juice, mashed	**14 oz.**	**398 mL**
Canned Romano beans, drained and mashed	**19 oz.**	**540 mL**
Bulgur	**⅔ cup**	**150 mL**
Ketchup	**2 tbsp.**	**30 mL**
Chili powder	**1 tbsp.**	**15 mL**
Salt	**1 tsp.**	**5 mL**
Pepper	**¼ tsp.**	**1 mL**
CRUST		
Yellow cornmeal	**1 cup**	**250 mL**
Baking powder	**1 tsp.**	**5 mL**
Salt	**½ tsp.**	**2 mL**
Large egg, fork-beaten	**1**	**1**
Milk	**¾ cup**	**175 mL**
Cooking oil	**2 tbsp.**	**30 mL**

Heat cooking oil in frying pan. Add onion, green pepper and garlic. Sauté until soft.

Add next 7 ingredients. Heat and stir until mixture boils. Cover and boil slowly for about 15 minutes. Stir often to keep from burning. It is quite thick. Turn into ungreased 8 × 8 inch (20 × 20 cm) pan. Set aside.

Crust: Stir cornmeal, baking powder and salt together in bowl. Add egg, milk and cooking oil. Stir. Pour over top. Bake, uncovered, in 350°F (175°C) oven for about 35 minutes until firm. Serves 6.

1 serving contains: *336 Calories (1405 kJ); 10.2 g Fat; 12 g Protein; 13 g Fiber*

Paré Pointer

With so many rocks in its bed the sea is bound to be restless.

VEGETABLE PIE

Each wedge contains a hard-boiled egg and creamy vegetables.

Sliced carrots	**1 cup**	**250 mL**
Sliced onion	**1 cup**	**250 mL**
Sliced celery	**1/2 cup**	**125 mL**
Cubed potato	**1 cup**	**250 mL**
Cubed turnip	**1/2 cup**	**125 mL**
Boiling water		
Frozen peas	**1 cup**	**250 mL**
SAUCE		
Butter or hard margarine	**3 tbsp.**	**50 mL**
All-purpose flour	**3 tbsp.**	**50 mL**
Instant vegetable stock mix	**2 tsp.**	**10 mL**
Salt	**1/2 tsp.**	**2 mL**
Pepper	**1/4 tsp.**	**1 mL**
Parsley flakes	**1 tsp.**	**5 mL**
Milk	**1 1/2 cups**	**375 mL**
Whole Wheat Pastry, page 106, enough for 2 crust, 9 inch (22 cm) pie		
Hard-boiled eggs	**6**	**6**

Cook first 5 vegetables in boiling water until tender.

Add peas. Cook for 2 or 3 minutes. Drain. Cool.

Sauce: Melt butter in saucepan. Mix in flour, vegetable stock mix, salt, pepper and parsley. Stir in milk until mixture boils and thickens. Cool. Mix sauce with vegetables.

Roll out pastry and line 9 inch (22 cm) pie plate. Spoon vegetables into pie shell.

Nestle eggs, spacing evenly lengthwise around edge, keeping about 1 inch (2.5 cm) in from edge. Roll out pastry for second crust. Dampen edges of bottom crust. Cover with top crust. Trim and crimp to seal. Cut slits in top. Bake in 400°F (205°C) oven for about 35 minutes until browned. Cut between mounds to serve 6.

1 serving contains: *593 Calories (2480 kJ); 37.2 g Fat; 16 g Protein; 6 g Fiber*

Pictured on page 143.

BUTTERSCOTCH PIE

Smooth and rich-tasting.

Cottage cheese, sieved or blended	**1 cup**	**250 mL**
Milk	**2 cups**	**425 mL**
Instant butterscotch pudding powder, 4 serving size each	**2**	**2**
Baked Oatmeal Pie Shell, page 98	**1**	**1**
Frozen whipped topping, thawed	**2 cups**	**500 mL**

Combine first 3 ingredients in bowl. Beat until smooth.

Pour into pie shell. Chill until firm.

Spread with topping. Cuts into 8 wedges.

1 wedge contains: *373 Calories (1559 kJ); 15.9 g Fat; 11 g Protein; 3 g Fiber*

VANILLA PIE: Substitute same quantity instant vanilla pudding powder for instant butterscotch pudding powder.

CHOCOLATE PIE: Substitute same quantity instant chocolate pudding powder for instant butterscotch pudding powder.

He thought he was dying so he went into the living room.

WHOLE WHEAT PASTRY

Even in pie crust you can get the benefit of whole wheat flour.

All-purpose flour	**1¼ cups**	**300 mL**
Whole wheat flour (see Note)	**1¼ cups**	**300 mL**
Brown sugar, packed	**1 tbsp.**	**15 mL**
Salt	**1 tsp.**	**5 mL**
Baking powder	**½ tsp.**	**2 mL**
Vegetable shortening	**1 cup**	**250 mL**
Water	**½ cup**	**125 mL**

Measure first 5 ingredients into bowl. Stir. Cut in shortening until mealy.

Sprinkle with water. Stir until you can work into a ball. Makes enough for 3 pie shells or casserole tops.

1 pie shell contains: *1036 Calories (4338 kJ); 73.7 g Fat; 13 g Protein; 8 g Fiber*

Note: All-purpose flour can be substituted for whole wheat flour.

1. Simple Rice Pot, page 138
2. Chick Pea Patties, page 77
3. Overnight Bean Salad, page 114
4. Cheesy Patties, page 93
5. Oatmeal Burgers, page 91
6. Legume Patties, page 78

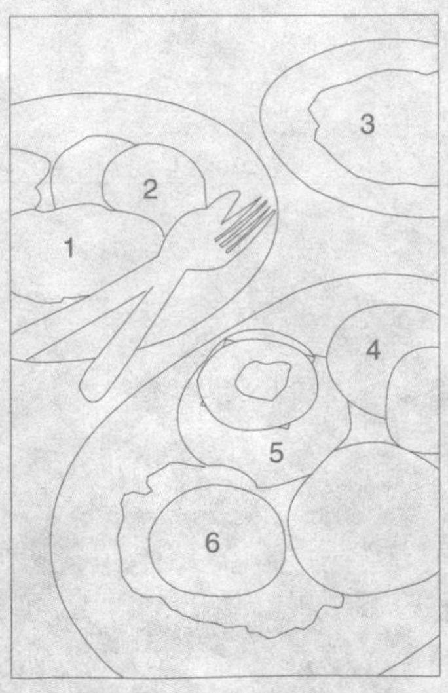

Dinner Plates Courtesy Of:
The Bay

Platter Courtesy Of:
Enchanted Kitchen

Flatware Courtesy Of:
IKEA

Cheesecake and pie all in one. Although the cheesecake starts out on the bottom, it rises to the occasion and ends up on top. Luscious.

Cream cheese, softened	**8 oz.**	**250 g**
Granulated sugar	**⅓ cup**	**75 mL**
Large egg	**1**	**1**
Vanilla	**1 tsp.**	**5 mL**
Salt	**¼ tsp.**	**1 mL**
Whole Wheat Pastry pie shell, page 106, 9 inch (22 cm), unbaked	**1**	**1**
Large eggs	**2**	**2**
Granulated sugar	**¼ cup**	**60 mL**
Corn syrup	**⅔ cup**	**150 mL**
Vanilla	**1 tsp.**	**5 mL**
Pecans, halves or chopped	**1 cup**	**250 mL**

Beat first 5 ingredients together well in bowl.

Pour into pie shell.

Beat eggs in bowl until frothy. Beat in second amount of sugar, corn syrup and vanilla.

Sprinkle pecans over cheese mixture. Pour syrup mixture over top. Bake in 375°F (190°C) oven for about 50 minutes. Cuts into 8 wedges.

1 wedge contains: *517 Calories (2161 kJ); 32.4 g Fat; 8 g Protein; 2 g Fiber*

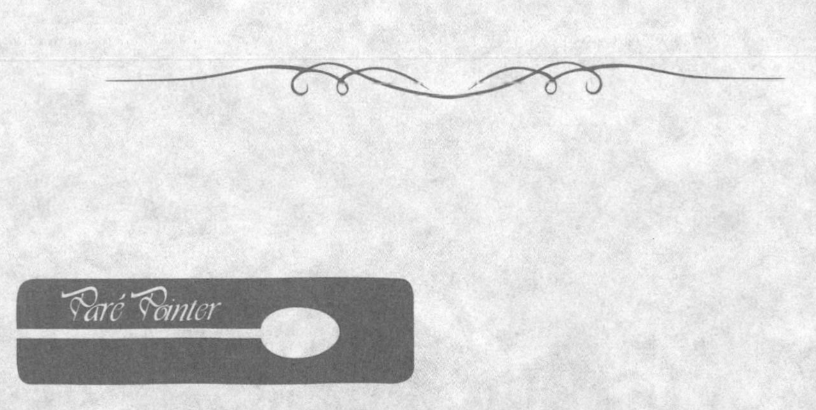

That executive is so efficient, he once went on a two week diet and ate everything in three days.

PASTA SALAD

Broccoli and grated cheese cheer up this salad with green and gold.

Elbow macaroni	**2 cups**	**500 mL**
Boiling water	**3 qts.**	**3 L**
Cooking oil (optional)	**1 tbsp.**	**15 mL**
Salt	**2 tsp.**	**10 mL**
Broccoli, cut bite size	**3 cups**	**750 mL**
Sliced green onion	**3 tbsp.**	**50 mL**
Grated medium or sharp Cheddar cheese	**1 cup**	**250 mL**
Grated Monterey Jack cheese	**1 cup**	**250 mL**
Sliced fresh mushrooms	**1 cup**	**250 mL**
Toasted sesame seeds	**3 tbsp.**	**50 mL**
DRESSING		
Red wine vinegar	**1/4 cup**	**60 mL**
Prepared mustard	**4 tsp.**	**20 mL**
Liquid honey	**4 tsp.**	**20 mL**
Soy sauce	**1 tsp.**	**5 mL**

Cook macaroni in boiling water, cooking oil and salt in large uncovered saucepan for 6 to 8 minutes until tender but firm. Drain. Rinse in cold water. Drain again well. Pour into large bowl.

Add next 6 ingredients. Stir lightly.

Dressing: Mix all 4 ingredients well in small bowl. Pour over salad. Toss to mix. Makes 8 cups (2 L).

1 cup (250 mL) contains: *255 Calories (1068 kJ); 11.0 g Fat; 12 g Protein; 2 g Fiber*

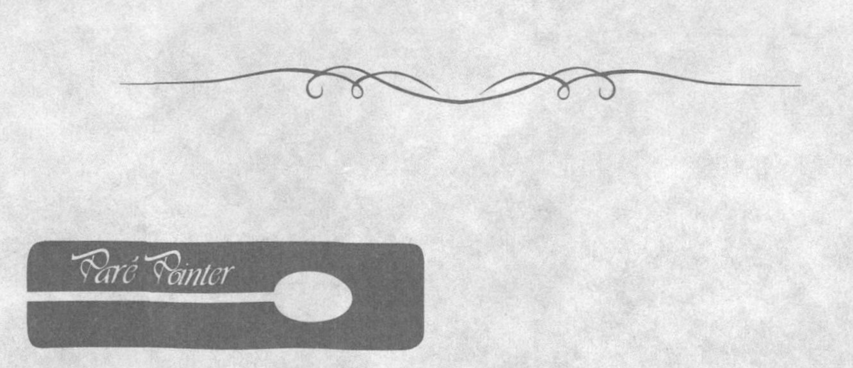

When kids have to go to school they're taut like a rope.

PASTA VEGGIE SALAD

Radiatore is such a uniquely shaped pasta. Several colors. A good, chunky, light-flavored salad.

Radiatore (or ½ lb., 227 g, other pasta)	**3 cups**	**750 mL**
Boiling water	**3 qts.**	**3 L**
Cooking oil (optional)	**1 tbsp.**	**15 mL**
Salt	**2 tsp.**	**10 mL**
Cauliflower, cut in small pieces	**2 cups**	**500 mL**
Broccoli, cut in small pieces	**2 cups**	**500 mL**
Grated carrot	**1 cup**	**250 mL**
Red pepper, chopped	**1**	**1**
Yellow pepper, chopped	**1**	**1**
Boiling water, to cover		
Salt	**1 tsp.**	**5 mL**
Chopped green onion	**¼ cup**	**60 mL**
Toasted sliced almonds	**¼ cup**	**60 mL**
DRESSING		
Red wine vinegar	**⅓ cup**	**75 mL**
Granulated sugar	**2 tbsp.**	**30 mL**
Dill weed	**½ tsp.**	**2 mL**
Garlic powder	**¼ tsp.**	**1 mL**
Cooking oil	**2 tbsp.**	**30 mL**

Cook radiatore in first amount of boiling water, cooking oil and salt in large uncovered saucepan for 9 to 11 minutes until tender but firm. Drain. Rinse in cold water. Drain well. Turn into large bowl.

Cook cauliflower, broccoli, carrot and red and yellow peppers in second amount of boiling water and salt for about 3 minutes until softened slightly but still crisp. Drain. Rinse in cold water. Drain well. Add to pasta.

Add onion and almonds.

Dressing: Mix first 4 ingredients well in small bowl. Stir until sugar dissolves.

Pour cooking oil over pasta mixture. Toss to coat. Pour dressing over top. Toss to mix. Makes about 10 cups (2.5 L).

***1 cup (250 mL) contains:** 156 Calories (652 kJ); 4.8 g Fat; 5 g Protein; 2 g Fiber*

Pictured on page 89.

PASTA VEGGIE CHEESE SALAD: To make this more of a meal-type salad, mix in 1 cup (250 mL) cubed mild or medium Cheddar cheese. Add a dinner roll and you're set.

TABBOULEH

A salad from the Middle East. Mint may be adjusted to suit your taste. Also good without mint.

Bulgur, fine grind	**1 cup**	**250 mL**
Boiling water	**1 cup**	**250 mL**
Medium tomatoes, diced	**3**	**3**
Green onions, chopped	**3**	**3**
Finely chopped fresh parsley, stems removed	**1½ tsp.**	**7 mL**
Chopped fresh mint (or 2 tsp., 10 mL, dried)	**1-2 tbsp.**	**15-30 mL**
Salt	**1 tsp.**	**5 mL**
Pepper	**¼ tsp.**	**1 mL**
Ground allspice	**⅛ tsp.**	**0.5 mL**
Olive oil (or cooking oil)	**¼ cup**	**60 mL**
Lemon juice, fresh or bottled	**2 tbsp.**	**30 mL**

Soak bulgur in boiling water for 15 minutes in large bowl. Cover bowl during soaking period.

Add remaining ingredients. Toss well. Makes 3 cups (750 mL).

½ cup (125 mL) contains: *186 Calories (777 kJ); 10.2 g Fat; 4 g Protein; 5 g Fiber*

Pictured on front cover.

APPLE ONION SALAD

A chunky salad. Red onion adds color and a mild onion flavor.

Medium red onion, chopped bite size	**1**	**1**
Water, to cover		
Salad dressing (or mayonnaise)	**⅔ cup**	**150 mL**
Commercial coleslaw dressing	**⅓ cup**	**75 mL**
Medium cooking apples, peeled and cut bite size (McIntosh is good)	**4**	**4**
Paprika, sprinkle		

(continued on next page)

Put onion into medium bowl. Add water. Let stand for 30 minutes. Drain in sieve for 5 minutes. Blot dry with paper towels.

Stir both dressings together in large bowl.

As you peel and cut apples, stir them into dressing so they don't darken. Add onion. Stir. Turn into bowl.

Sprinkle with paprika. Makes 6 cups (1.35 L).

1 cup (250 mL) contains: *261 Calories (1091 kJ); 20.5 g Fat; 1 g Protein; 2 g Fiber*

BEET SALAD

Unusual and very tasty.

Lemon-flavored gelatin (jelly powder)	**1 × 3 oz.**	**1 × 85 g**
Boiling water	**1 cup**	**250 mL**
White vinegar	**3 tbsp.**	**50 mL**
Prepared horseradish	**2 tsp.**	**10 mL**
Salt	**1 tsp.**	**5 mL**
Onion powder	**1/4 tsp.**	**1 mL**
Grated cabbage	**1 1/2 cups**	**375 mL**
Cooked diced beets, patted dry with paper towel	**1 cup**	**250 mL**
Diced red or green pepper	**1/4 cup**	**60 mL**
Diced celery	**1/4 cup**	**60 mL**
Cucumber slices, paper thin, for garnish		

Stir gelatin into boiling water in bowl until dissolved.

Add vinegar, horseradish, salt and onion powder. Stir. Chill, stirring and scraping down sides of bowl, until mixture begins to thicken.

Fold in cabbage, beets, pepper and celery. Turn into 3 cup (750 mL) mold. Chill.

Unmold salad onto plate. Garnish with cucumber slices. Makes 3 cups (750 mL).

1/2 cup (125 mL) contains: *71 Calories (295 kJ); trace Fat; 2 g Protein; 1 g Fiber*

OVERNIGHT BEAN SALAD

Crunchy, colorful, good flavor and a real lifesaver to have on hand. Keeps for weeks in the refrigerator.

Canned yellow wax beans, drained	**14 oz.**	**398 mL**
Canned cut green beans, drained	**14 oz.**	**398 mL**
Canned kidney beans, drained	**14 oz.**	**398 mL**
Canned chick peas (garbanzo beans), drained	**19 oz.**	**540 mL**
Large onion, sliced	**1**	**1**
Red pepper, sliced in strips	**1**	**1**
DRESSING		
Granulated sugar	**1 cup**	**250 mL**
Red wine vinegar	**¾ cup**	**175 mL**
Cooking oil	**2 tbsp.**	**30 mL**
Salt	**1 tsp.**	**5 mL**
Pepper	**½ tsp.**	**2 mL**

Combine first 6 ingredients in bowl.

Dressing: Stir all 5 ingredients together well in separate bowl. Pour over bean mixture. Stir gently. Cover. Refrigerate overnight. Stir occasionally in evening and next morning. Makes 9 cups (2 L).

1 cup (250 mL) contains: *244 Calories (1023 kJ); 4.4 g Fat; 7 g Protein; 6 g Fiber*

Pictured on page 107.

SPINACH SALAD

Spinach and mushrooms are dressed with a tart yet sweet dressing.

Spinach leaves, torn bite size, lightly packed	**5 cups**	**1.25 L**
Sliced fresh mushrooms	**1 cup**	**250 mL**
DRESSING		
White vinegar	**2 tbsp.**	**30 mL**
Granulated sugar	**1 tbsp.**	**15 mL**
Prepared mustard	**¼ tsp.**	**1 mL**
Garlic powder	**1/16 tsp.**	**0.5 mL**
Cooking oil	**2 tsp.**	**10 mL**

(continued on next page)

Place spinach and mushrooms in large bowl.

Dressing: Stir first 4 ingredients together in small bowl until sugar is dissolved.

Pour cooking oil over salad in bowl. Toss to coat. Pour dressing over top. Toss. Serves 4.

1 serving contains: *45 Calories (188 kJ); 2.5 g Fat; 1 g Protein; 1 g Fiber*

SPINACH BACON SALAD: Add 3 slices cooked veggie back bacon, slivered or chopped.

SLIVERED AND SLICED SALAD

A combination of vegetables and fruit with a tangy dressing.

HONEY MUSTARD DRESSING		
White vinegar	**¼ cup**	**60 mL**
Prepared mustard	**2 tsp.**	**10 mL**
Liquid honey	**¼ cup**	**60 mL**
Cornstarch	**2 tsp.**	**10 mL**
SALAD		
Sliced fresh mushrooms	**1½ cups**	**375 mL**
Canned French-style green beans, drained, blotted dry	**14 oz.**	**398 mL**
Green onions, sliced	**4**	**4**
Cherry tomatoes, halved	**6-10**	**6-10**
Oranges, peeled and divided into segments (navel is best)	**1-2**	**1-2**

Honey Mustard Dressing: Mix all 4 ingredients in saucepan. Heat and stir until mixture boils and thickens. Cool. Makes scant ½ cup (125 mL).

Salad: Toss mushrooms, beans and onion together in medium bowl. Add enough dressing to coat, about 2 tbsp. (30 mL). Toss. Pile down center of serving plate.

Cluster cherry tomatoes on 1 side of mushroom mixture and orange segments on other side. Drizzle dressing over top. Serves 8 as a side salad.

1 serving contains: *63 Calories (264 kJ); trace Fat; 1 g Protein; 2 g Fiber*

Pictured on page 125.

CORN CHIP SALAD

Crunchy with the taste of corn chips. Chili powder adds an extra touch along with the dressing.

Small head of lettuce, cut or torn	**1**	**1**
Grated medium or sharp Cheddar cheese	**2 cups**	**500 mL**
Medium tomatoes, diced and drained on paper towel	**2**	**2**
Green onions, sliced	**3-4**	**3-4**
Canned ranch-style beans (or kidney beans), drained and rinsed	**½ × 14 oz.**	**½ × 398 mL**
Chili powder	**1 tsp.**	**5 mL**

ISLAND DRESSING

Cooking oil	**1 tbsp.**	**15 mL**
All-purpose flour	**1 tbsp.**	**15 mL**
Water	**3 tbsp.**	**50 mL**
White vinegar	**2 tbsp.**	**30 mL**
Granulated sugar	**¼ cup**	**60 mL**
Ketchup	**2 tsp.**	**10 mL**
Onion powder	**⅛ tsp.**	**0.5 mL**
Salt	**⅛ tsp.**	**0.5 mL**
Corn chips	**3 cups**	**750 mL**

Combine first 6 ingredients in large bowl. Toss.

Island Dressing: Stir cooking oil and flour together in small saucepan.

Stir in remaining ingredients. Heat and stir until mixture boils and thickens. Cool thoroughly before using. Makes ½ cup (125 mL). Add to salad. Toss well to coat. Chill for 30 minutes.

Add corn chips just before serving. Toss. Makes 10 cups (2.5 L).

1 cup (250 mL) contains: *267 Calories (1119 kJ); 15.3 g Fat; 9 g Protein; 3 g Fiber*

Pictured on page 71.

CABBAGE SALAD

Colorful and crunchy. A variety salad with good taste appeal. A new twist on coleslaw.

Shredded cabbage, packed	**4 cups**	**1 L**
Grated carrot	**½ cup**	**125 mL**
Finely chopped green onion	**¼ cup**	**60 mL**
Shelled sunflower seeds	**⅓ cup**	**75 mL**
Bean sprouts	**½ cup**	**125 mL**
Raisins	**¼ cup**	**60 mL**
DRESSING		
Salad dressing (or mayonnaise)	**½ cup**	**125 mL**
Plain yogurt	**½ cup**	**125 mL**
White vinegar	**2 tbsp.**	**30 mL**
Granulated sugar	**2 tsp.**	**10 mL**

Toss first 6 ingredients in large bowl to mix.

Dressing: Stir all ingredients together. Pour over salad. Toss well to coat. Makes 4½ cups (1.1 L).

½ cup (125 mL) contains: *137 Calories (575 kJ); 9.5 g Fat; 2 g Protein; 1 g Fiber*

BEAN SANDWICH

So much protein. So little cost.

Canned white or pinto beans, drained	**14 oz.**	**398 mL**
Sweet pickle relish	**2 tbsp.**	**30 mL**
Salad dressing (or mayonnaise)	**2 tbsp.**	**30 mL**
Chili sauce (or ketchup)	**1 tbsp.**	**15 mL**

Combine all 4 ingredients in small bowl. Mash. Bottom of drinking glass works well. Makes about 1⅓ cups (325 mL) filling.

⅓ cup (75 mL) contains: *142 Calories (596 kJ); 4.1 g Fat; 6 g Protein; 3 g Fiber*

AVIAL

An East Indian dish from the southern region. Good flavor and colorful vegetables. a-VEE-yahl can be eaten with rice.

Vegetables such as green beans, potatoes, carrots, kohlrabi, green plantain, cubed	**4 cups**	**1 L**
Water	**2 cups**	**500 mL**
Salt	**1 tsp.**	**5 mL**
Water	**2 tbsp.**	**30 mL**
Canned chopped green chilies, drained (see Note)	**4 oz.**	**114 mL**
Chopped fresh coriander, packed	**1 tbsp.**	**15 mL**
Ginger paste	**1 tsp.**	**5 mL**
Coconut powder or fine coconut (see Note)	**1/2 cup**	**125 mL**
Cumin seeds	**1 tsp.**	**5 mL**
Turmeric	**1/4 tsp.**	**1 mL**
Cayenne pepper (Indian chili powder)	**1/8-1/4 tsp.**	**0.5-1 mL**
Plain yogurt	**1/3 cup**	**75 mL**
Indian bread (such as roti or chapati) or steamed rice		

Cook vegetables in water and salt in saucepan for about 10 minutes until tender. Drain.

Grind next 8 ingredients into a paste in blender. Add to vegetables. Cool.

Stir in yogurt.

Serve with roti or chapati, or with rice. Makes 2 1/2 cups (625 mL).

1/2 cup (125 mL) contains: *160 Calories (671 kJ); 6.8 g Fat; 4 g Protein; 3 g Fiber*

Note: Chopped green chilies and cayenne pepper can be omitted and 2 hot chopped green peppers added. Coconut powder gives better flavor than fine coconut.

Paré Pointer

A jeweler sells watches and a jailer watches cells.

PROTEIN BURGERS

Basil adds to the flavor of these. A slightly chewy texture.

Boiling water	**1/4 cup**	**60 mL**
Bulgur	**1/4 cup**	**60 mL**
Red lentils	**3 tbsp.**	**50 mL**
Boiling water, to cover		
Cooked dried navy beans (measure after cooking), see Note	**1 3/4 cups**	**425 mL**
Butter or hard margarine	**1 1/2 tbsp.**	**25 mL**
Chopped onion	**1 1/4 cups**	**300 mL**
Dried sweet basil	**1 tsp.**	**5 mL**
Salt	**3/4 tsp.**	**4 mL**
Pepper	**1/8 tsp.**	**0.5 mL**
Garlic powder	**1/4 tsp.**	**1 mL**
Gravy browner	**1 tsp.**	**5 mL**
Hamburger buns, split and buttered	**8**	**8**

Pour first amount of boiling water over bulgur in small bowl. Cover. Let stand 15 minutes.

Cook lentils in second amount of boiling water until tender. Drain.

Add beans to lentils. Mash with bottom of drinking glass.

Heat butter in frying pan. Add onion. Sauté until soft. Turn into separate bowl.

Add remaining ingredients. Mix. Add bulgur mixture and lentil mixture. Mix well. Shape into patties using about 1/4 cup (60 mL) each. Brown both sides in greased frying pan.

Insert patties into buns. Serve as burgers with all the trimmings. Makes 8 burgers.

1 burger contains: *260 Calories (1087 kJ); 5.4 g Fat; 10 g Protein; 4 g Fiber*

Note: Canned navy beans may be substituted if you don't have any cooked beans on hand. Use 14 oz. (398 mL).

MUSHROOM BURGERS

Excellent texture, flavor and appearance. Good with or without cheese.

Large eggs	**2**	**2**
Finely chopped onion	**½ cup**	**125 mL**
Chopped fresh mushrooms	**2 cups**	**500 mL**
Fine dry bread crumbs	**½ cup**	**125 mL**
All-purpose flour	**¼ cup**	**60 mL**
Salt	**1 tsp.**	**5 mL**
Pepper	**¼ tsp.**	**1 mL**
Ground thyme	**¼ tsp.**	**1 mL**
Grated medium or sharp Cheddar cheese (optional)	**½ cup**	**125 mL**
Hamburger buns, split and buttered	**8**	**8**

Whisk eggs in bowl. Stir in onion and mushrooms.

Add next 6 ingredients. Mix well. Shape into patties using ¼ cup (60 mL) for each. Cook in greased frying pan browning both sides.

Insert patties into buns. Serve with condiments. Makes 8 burgers.

1 burger contains: *235 Calories (983 kJ); 6.7 g Fat; 9 g Protein; 2 g Fiber*

OVEN SUBS

These appetizing buns make a good quick lunch.

Submarine buns (or hamburger buns)	**4**	**4**
Butter or hard margarine	**1 tbsp.**	**15 mL**
Chopped onion	**1¼ cups**	**300 mL**
Canned beans in tomato sauce	**14 oz.**	**398 mL**
Ketchup	**1 tbsp.**	**15 mL**
Salt, sprinkle		
Pepper, sprinkle		
Grated medium or sharp Cheddar cheese	**¾ cup**	**175 mL**

(continued on next page)

Cut each bun horizontally in half.

Melt butter in frying pan. Add onion. Sauté until soft.

Add beans, ketchup, salt and pepper. Stir. Spread bottom halves of buns with mixture.

Top mixture with cheese. Replace top halves of buns. Wrap each bun in foil. Bake in 350°F (175°C) oven for 15 minutes until hot. Makes a generous 2 cups (500 mL) filling, enough for 4 sub sandwiches.

1 sandwich contains: *513 Calories (2147 kJ); 16.6 g Fat; 19 g Protein; 9 g Fiber*

BEAN BURGERS

Sensational with fried onion.

Canned beans in tomato sauce	**14 oz.**	**398 mL**
Grated sharp Cheddar cheese	**¾ cup**	**175 mL**
Dry bread crumbs	**1½ cups**	**375 mL**
Large egg	**1**	**1**
Gravy browner	**1 tsp.**	**5 mL**
Soy sauce	**2 tsp.**	**10 mL**
Bulgur	**¼ cup**	**60 mL**
Boiling water	**¼ cup**	**60 mL**
Cooking oil	**1 tbsp.**	**15 mL**
Hamburger buns, split and buttered	**8**	**8**
Onion, sliced and fried	**1**	**1**
Ketchup		
Relish		

Mash beans in bowl.

Mix in cheese, bread crumbs, egg, gravy browner and soy sauce. Let stand 10 minutes.

Combine bulgur and boiling water in small bowl. Cover. Let stand 15 minutes. Add to bean mixture. Shape into patties about ¼ cup (60 mL) each.

Heat cooking oil in frying pan. Add patties. Brown on both sides.

Insert patties into buns. Add onion, ketchup and relish. Makes 10.

1 burger contains: *292 Calories (1222 kJ); 8.2 g Fat; 11 g Protein; 4 g Fiber*

CLUB SANDWICH

Yes, it's possible to make party sandwiches from club sandwiches. Use them for a meal as well.

Whole wheat bread slices, buttered	**3**	**3**
Egg Filling, page 129	**⅓ cup**	**75 mL**
Veggie "meat" slices	**3**	**3**
Lettuce leaves	**3**	**3**
White bread slices, buttered	**3**	**3**
Veggie "meat" slices, or other	**3**	**3**
Tomato slices	**6**	**6**
Cucumber slices, paper thin	**12**	**12**
Salt, sprinkle		
Pepper, sprinkle		
Whole wheat bread slices, buttered	**3**	**3**

Lay 3 slices whole wheat bread on working surface. Cover each with egg filling, 1 veggie "meat" slice and 1 lettuce leaf.

Butter second sides of white bread. Lay over lettuce. Add slice of same or different "meat" slice to each. Top each with tomato slices and cucumber slices. Sprinkle with salt and pepper.

Add second slices of whole wheat bread, buttered side down. Cut off crusts. Cut each sandwich into 3 fingers. Makes 9 attractive sandwiches.

1 sandwich contains: *108 Calories (444 kJ); 2.4 g Fat; 7 g Protein; 2 g Fiber*

If you sing while driving to work you have a car-tune.

FAJITAS

It's all here—veggies and "meat" strips rolled in tortillas. A sweet and sour flavor.

Cooking oil	**1 tbsp.**	**15 mL**
Thinly sliced onion	**1½ cups**	**375 mL**
Large green pepper, thinly sliced into long matchsticks	**1**	**1**
Medium potatoes, cut as for French fries	**2**	**2**
Boiling water, to cover		
Flour tortillas, 8 inch (20 cm) size	**6**	**6**
Canned diced green chilies, drained	**4 oz.**	**114 mL**
White vinegar	**2 tbsp.**	**30 mL**
Liquid honey	**2 tsp.**	**10 mL**
Garlic powder	**½ tsp.**	**2 mL**
Ground coriander	**¼ tsp.**	**1 mL**
Ground cumin	**¼ tsp.**	**1 mL**
Salt	**¼ tsp.**	**1 mL**
Pepper	**⅛ tsp.**	**0.5 mL**
Tofu wieners, cut in thick matchsticks	**6**	**6**
Sour cream, guacamole, salsa and grated cheese of your choice		

Heat cooking oil in frying pan. Add onion and green pepper. Sauté until soft. Remove from heat.

Cook potato in boiling water until tender-crisp when pierced with tip of paring knife. Drain. Add to onion mixture.

Wrap tortillas in foil. Heat in 350°F (175°C) oven for 8 to 10 minutes.

Add next 8 ingredients to onion mixture. Heat slowly, stirring gently once or twice, until hot.

Add wieners. Heat through. Turn out onto warmed platter. Open foil on tortillas.

Have people build their own using condiments as go-withs. Makes 6 fajitas.

***1 fajita contains:** 261 Calories (1094 kJ); 3.2 g Fat; 17 g Protein; 2 g Fiber*

MEATLESS BURGERS

Use in your favorite bun. Could almost pass for a chicken burger.

Creamed cottage cheese	**¾ cup**	**175 mL**
Rolled oats (not instant)	**⅔ cup**	**150 mL**
Dry bread or cracker crumbs	**⅓ cup**	**75 mL**
Garlic salt	**¼ tsp.**	**1 mL**
Onion powder	**¼ tsp.**	**1 mL**
Ground walnuts (or other nuts)	**½ cup**	**125 mL**
Large egg	**1**	**1**
Evaporated milk (or light cream)	**⅓ cup**	**75 mL**
Soy sauce	**¼ tsp.**	**1 mL**
Cooking oil	**1 tbsp.**	**15 mL**

Place first 6 ingredients in bowl. Mix well.

Beat egg in small bowl. Add milk and soy sauce. Beat to mix. Pour into cottage cheese mixture. Stir. Let stand at least 10 minutes. Shape into patties using about ¼ cup (60 mL) for each.

Heat cooking oil in frying pan. Brown patties on both sides. Makes 6.

1 serving contains: *185 Calories (774 kJ); 10.4 g Fat; 9 g Protein; 1 g Fiber*

1. Falafels, page 127
2. Tahini Sauce, page 130
3. Slivered And Sliced Salad, page 115
4. Vegetable Pizza, page 98

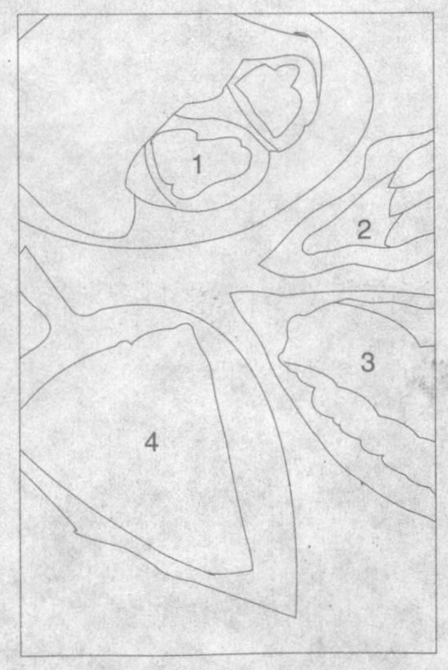

Serving Plates Courtesy Of:
The Bay

Wire Serving Basket Courtesy Of:
Chintz & Company

Serving Tongs And Linens Courtesy Of:
La Cache

FALAFELS

Make medium feh-LAH-fehl patties or balls to stuff a pita or make small balls for an appetizer.

Canned chick peas (garbanzo beans), drained	**19 oz.**	**540 mL**
Chopped onion	**3/4 cup**	**175 mL**
Ground cumin	**3/4 tsp.**	**4 mL**
Garlic powder	**1/2 tsp.**	**2 mL**
Parsley flakes	**1/2 tsp.**	**2 mL**
Baking powder	**1/2 tsp.**	**2 mL**
Salt	**3/4 tsp.**	**4 mL**
Pepper	**1/4 tsp.**	**1 mL**
Ground coriander	**1/2 tsp.**	**2 mL**
Turmeric	**1/8 tsp.**	**0.5 mL**
Fine dry bread crumbs	**1 cup**	**250 mL**
Large eggs	**2**	**2**
Cooking oil, for deep-frying		
Pitas	**11**	**11**
Tahini Sauce, page 130		

Run chick peas and onion through food grinder or food processor.

Add next 10 ingredients. Mix well. Shape into 1 inch (2.5 cm) balls. Leave balls round or flatten them into patties.

Lower balls or patties on slotted spoon into hot 375°F (190°C) cooking oil. Cook about 45 seconds or until the desired shade of brown. Remove with slotted spoon to dish lined with paper towel.

Stuff pitas using 4 balls or flattened patties in each. Spoon Tahini Sauce over falafels. Makes 44 falafels, enough for 11 pitas.

1 pita plus 4 falafels contains: *342 Calories (1432 kJ); 10.1 g Fat; 11 g Protein; 2 g Fiber*

Pictured on page 125.

FALAFEL APPETIZERS: Shape into 3/4 inch (2 cm) balls. Serve hot with picks on the side with Tahini Sauce for dipping. Makes about 65.

MAIN FALAFELS: Shape into 1 1/2 inch (4 cm) balls to serve for a main course. Serve with Tahini Sauce. Makes about 22.

BURRITOS

These are flavorful on their own but with salsa and sour cream they are extra good and spiced just right.

Cooking oil	**2 tsp.**	**10 mL**
Chopped onion	**1¼ cups**	**300 mL**
Garlic cloves, minced (or ½ tsp., 2 mL, garlic powder)	**2**	**2**
Medium potatoes, quartered	**2**	**2**
Boiling water, to cover		
Canned kidney beans (or pinto beans), drained	**14 oz.**	**398 mL**
Whole oregano	**½ tsp.**	**2 mL**
Ground cumin	**½ tsp.**	**2 mL**
Salt	**½ tsp.**	**2 mL**
Pepper	**⅛ tsp.**	**0.5 mL**
Flour tortillas, 8 inch (20 cm)	**6**	**6**
Salsa (mild, medium or hot)		
Sour cream		

Heat cooking oil in frying pan. Add onion and garlic. Sauté until soft and golden. Remove from heat.

Cook potatoes in boiling water until tender-crisp when pierced with tip of paring knife. Cool enough to handle. Cut into small dice. Add to onion.

Empty kidney beans into shallow pan or bowl. Add oregano, cumin, salt and pepper. Using bottom of water glass, mash well. Add to onion. Heat onion mixture, stirring often.

Wrap tortillas in foil. Heat in 350°F (175°C) oven for 8 to 10 minutes. Divide bean mixture down centers of tortillas. Fold 1 side over, then ends, then roll. Filling should be completely enclosed. If not serving immediately, wrap in foil and place in 200°F (95°C) oven.

Serve with salsa and sour cream. Makes 6 burritos.

1 burrito contains: *240 Calories (1005 kJ); 2.5 g Fat; 9 g Protein; 6 g Fiber*

EGG FILLING

Mild flavored. Handy to have in the refrigerator.

Hard-boiled eggs, mashed	**2**	**2**
Salad dressing (or mayonnaise)	**1 tsp.**	**5 mL**
Milk	**1 tbsp.**	**15 mL**
Salt, sprinkle		
Pepper, sprinkle		
Prepared mustard	**½ tsp.**	**2 mL**
Chopped chives	**1 tsp.**	**5 mL**
White vinegar	**½ tsp.**	**2 mL**

Mix all ingredients well in small bowl. Taste for salt and pepper, adding more if needed. Makes a generous ⅓ cup (75 mL), enough to thinly cover 3 slices of bread, such as for Club Sandwich, page 122.

***1½ tbsp. (25 mL) contain:** 63 Calories (265 kJ); 4.5 g Fat; 4 g Protein; trace Fiber*

TACOS

A great do-it-yourself meal. Just fill your taco shell with layers.

Canned refried beans	**14 oz.**	**398 mL**
Salsa (mild, medium or hot)	**¼ cup**	**60 mL**
Chopped head lettuce	**1 cup**	**250 mL**
Tomato, diced	**1**	**1**
Red onion or other mild onion, cut in slivers (optional)	**1**	**1**
Grated mild or medium Cheddar cheese (or Monterey Jack cheese)	**½ cup**	**125 mL**
Sour cream (optional)	**6 tbsp.**	**100 mL**
Taco shells	**8-10**	**8-10**

Heat beans in heavy saucepan.

Place next 6 ingredients in separate containers ready to serve.

Divide beans among taco shells. Make additional layers of salsa, lettuce, tomato, onion, cheese and sour cream. Makes 10 tacos.

***1 taco contains:** 125 Calories (523 kJ); 4.5 g Fat; 5 g Protein; 3 g Fiber*

RED SAUCE

Good color. Flavorful without being too sharp. Serve with Cheesy Nut Bake, page 85.

Butter or hard margarine	**3 tbsp.**	**50 mL**
Chopped onion	**1½ cups**	**375 mL**
Medium green pepper, seeded and cut in short slivers	**1**	**1**
Sliced fresh mushrooms	**1 cup**	**250 mL**
Canned tomatoes, with juice, broken up	**14 oz.**	**398 mL**
Water	**1 cup**	**250 mL**
Small bay leaf	**1**	**1**
Salt	**½ tsp.**	**2 mL**
Pepper	**¼ tsp.**	**1 mL**
Instant vegetable stock mix	**2 tsp.**	**10 mL**
Garlic powder	**⅛ tsp.**	**0.5 mL**
Ground thyme, just a pinch		
Granulated sugar	**½ tsp.**	**2 mL**

Melt butter in frying pan. Add onion and green pepper. Sauté until soft.

Add mushrooms. Sauté for 2 to 3 minutes.

Add remaining 9 ingredients. Stir. Simmer, covered, for 20 minutes, stirring occasionally. Discard bay leaf. Makes about 2 cups (500 mL).

½ cup (125 mL) contains: *146 Calories (609 kJ); 9.8 g Fat; 3 g Protein; 3 g Fiber*

Pictured on page 89.

TAHINI SAUCE

Serve as a dip for appetizers, as a spread in Falafels, page 127, or as a sauce with a snack or main course.

Tahini, page 49	**½ cup**	**125 mL**
Water	**⅓ cup**	**75 mL**
Lemon juice, fresh or bottled	**⅓ cup**	**75 mL**
Salt	**½ tsp.**	**2 mL**
Garlic powder	**¼-½ tsp.**	**1-2 mL**

Mix all 5 ingredients together in blender. Process until smooth. Makes 1 cup (250 mL).

2 tbsp. (30 mL) contain: *76 Calories (319 kJ); 7.0 g Fat; 2 g Protein; 1 g Fiber*

Pictured on page 125.

BROWN GRAVY

Enjoy gravy with your patties and cutlets.

Water	**$2\frac{1}{4}$ cups**	**560 mL**
All-purpose flour	**6 tbsp.**	**100 mL**
Instant vegetable stock mix	**$1\frac{1}{2}$ tsp.**	**7 mL**
Onion powder	**1 tsp.**	**5 mL**
Celery salt	**$\frac{1}{4}$ tsp.**	**1 mL**
Gravy browner	**$\frac{1}{2}$ tsp.**	**2 mL**
Water	**$\frac{3}{4}$ cup**	**175 mL**
Yeast extract (such as Marmite or Vegemite)	**1 tsp.**	**5 mL**
Salt	**$\frac{1}{4}$ tsp.**	**1 mL**
Pepper	**$\frac{1}{8}$ tsp.**	**0.5 mL**

Heat first amount of water in saucepan until it boils.

Mix next 9 ingredients in small bowl until smooth. Stir into boiling water until mixture returns to a boil and thickens. Makes $2\frac{2}{3}$ cups (575 mL).

***$\frac{1}{3}$ cup (75 mL) contains:** 28 Calories (115 kJ); trace Fat; 1 g Protein; trace Fiber*

PEANUT SAUCE

Make this as spicy hot as you like. Serve with Veggie Wraps, page 75.

Smooth peanut butter	**$\frac{3}{4}$ cup**	**175 mL**
Hot water	**$\frac{3}{4}$ cup**	**175 mL**
Cider vinegar	**2 tbsp.**	**30 mL**
Soy sauce	**4 tsp.**	**20 mL**
Mild molasses	**2 tsp.**	**10 mL**
Hot pepper sauce	**$\frac{1}{2}$-1 tsp.**	**2-5 mL**

Stir peanut butter and hot water in small bowl until smooth.

Add remaining ingredients. Stir. Makes $1\frac{1}{2}$ cups (350 mL).

***2 tbsp. (30 mL) contain:** 107 Calories (446 kJ); 8.7 g Fat; 4 g Protein; 1 g Fiber*

SPICY PEANUT DIP: For a highly spiced dip, add more hot pepper sauce to taste.

SPICY PEANUT DRESSING: To dress a green salad, stir in a bit of water to make a barely pourable dressing. Add more hot pepper sauce to taste, if desired.

MUSHROOM SAUCE

Pour over "meat" loaves, patties or balls to change into a party dish.

Butter or hard margarine	**¼ cup**	**60 mL**
All-purpose flour	**¼ cup**	**60 mL**
Salt	**½ tsp.**	**2 mL**
Pepper	**⅛ tsp.**	**0.5 mL**
Instant vegetable stock mix	**2 tsp.**	**10 mL**
Paprika	**½ tsp.**	**2 mL**
Water	**2 cups**	**500 mL**
Worcestershire sauce	**½ tsp.**	**2 mL**
Dry onion flakes	**2 tbsp.**	**30 mL**
Canned sliced mushrooms, drained	**10 oz.**	**284 mL**

Melt butter in saucepan. Mix in next 5 ingredients.

Stir in water, Worcestershire sauce and onion flakes until mixture boils and thickens.

Add mushrooms. Stir. Heat through. Makes a generous 2¼ cups (550 mL).

¼ cup (60 mL) contains: *80 Calories (334 kJ); 5.9 g Fat; 1 g Protein; 1 g Fiber*

Pictured on page 71.

SWEET AND SOUR SAUCE

Perfect to serve over "meatballs" or patties.

Brown sugar, packed	**1½ cups**	**375 mL**
All-purpose flour	**¼ cup**	**60 mL**
Water	**1¼ cups**	**300 mL**
White vinegar	**½ cup**	**125 mL**
Soy sauce	**1½ tbsp.**	**25 mL**
Ketchup	**1 tbsp.**	**15 mL**

Stir brown sugar and flour together in saucepan.

Mix in water slowly. Add vinegar, soy sauce and ketchup. Heat and stir until mixture boils and thickens. Makes about 2¼ cups (550 mL).

¼ cup (60 mL) contains: *164 Calories (685 kJ); trace Fat; 1 g Protein; trace Fiber*

PINTO TORTILLA SOUP

An excellent soup. Rich and hearty-looking. Mild salsa makes it spicy hot. A real winner.

Butter or hard margarine	**1 tbsp.**	**15 mL**
Chopped onion	**1/2 cup**	**125 mL**
Minced garlic	**1 tsp.**	**5 mL**
Water	**3 cups**	**750 mL**
Salsa, mild (or medium if you dare)	**3 cups**	**750 mL**
Canned pinto beans, with liquid	**2 × 14 oz.**	**2 × 398 mL**
Chopped red pepper	**1/2 cup**	**125 mL**
Bay leaf	**1**	**1**
Instant vegetable stock mix	**2 tbsp.**	**30 mL**
Pepper	**1/4 tsp.**	**1 mL**
GARNISH		
Flour tortillas, cut in 1 1/2 × 3/4 inch (4 × 2 cm) strips	**2-3**	**2-3**
Cooking oil, for deep-frying		
Grated medium Cheddar cheese or Monterey Jack cheese	**1/2 cup**	**125 mL**

Melt butter in saucepan. Add onion and garlic. Sauté until soft.

Add next 7 ingredients. Simmer, covered, for 1 hour. Discard bay leaf.

Garnish: Cook tortilla strips in hot 375°F (190°C) cooking oil until browned. Drain on paper towels.

Add some cheese and tortilla strips to each bowl of soup, if desired. Makes about 8 1/2 cups (2 L), enough for 8 servings.

1 serving contains: *181 Calories (757 kJ); 3.8 g Fat; 8 g Protein; 5 g Fiber*

Pictured on page 143.

MINESTRONE

A full soup that becomes a full meal when served with crusty rolls.

Water	**8 cups**	**2 L**
Canned tomatoes with juice, cut up	**14 oz.**	**398 mL**
Chopped onion	**2½ cups**	**625 mL**
Thinly sliced carrot	**1 cup**	**250 mL**
Thinly sliced celery	**¾ cup**	**175 mL**
Canned kidney beans, with liquid	**14 oz.**	**398 mL**
Cut green beans, fresh or frozen	**2 cups**	**500 mL**
Elbow macaroni, uncooked	**2 cups**	**500 mL**
Instant vegetable stock mix	**2 tbsp.**	**30 mL**
Parsley flakes	**2 tsp.**	**10 mL**
Salt	**1½ tsp.**	**7 mL**
Pepper	**¼ tsp.**	**1 mL**

Measure first 5 ingredients into Dutch oven. Heat, stirring often, until mixture comes to a boil. Cover. Simmer slowly for about 35 minutes until vegetables are cooked.

Add kidney beans and green beans. Return to a boil. Cook until green beans are tender.

Add macaroni, stock mix, parsley flakes, salt and pepper. Cover. Stir often as you return mixture to a boil. Cook for about 10 minutes until macaroni is tender but firm. Makes 13½ cups (3.37 L), enough for 12 servings.

1 serving contains: *140 Calories (586 kJ); 1.2 g Fat; 6 g Protein; 4 g Fiber*

Pictured on page 143.

PUMPKIN SOUP

Pumpkin-colored and pumpkin-flavored. Tasty.

Butter or hard margarine	**1 tbsp.**	**15 mL**
Chopped onion	**1 cup**	**250 mL**
Canned tomatoes with juice, mashed	**14 oz.**	**398 mL**
Canned pumpkin (without spice) or same quantity fresh, cooked and mashed	**14 oz.**	**398 mL**
Instant vegetable stock mix	**2 tbsp.**	**30 mL**
Water	**2 cups**	**500 mL**
Milk	**2 cups**	**500 mL**
Salt	**1½ tsp.**	**7 mL**
Pepper	**⅛-¼ tsp.**	**0.5-1 mL**

(continued on next page)

Melt butter in large saucepan or Dutch oven. Add onion. Sauté until soft.

Add remaining ingredients. Heat, stirring often, until very hot. Do not boil or it might curdle. Makes 7 cups (1.7 L).

1 cup (250 mL) contains: *111 Calories (466 kJ); 4.5 g Fat; 4 g Protein; 2 g Fiber*

Variation: Try adding 1/8 to 1/4 tsp. (0.5 to 1 mL) ground thyme for a great flavor.

GARBANZO SOUP

This has its own good flavor. Great choice.

Cooking oil	**2 tbsp.**	**30 mL**
Chopped onion	**1 1/2 cups**	**375 mL**
Canned tomatoes, with juice, broken up	**14 oz.**	**398 mL**
Ketchup	**2 tbsp.**	**30 mL**
Instant vegetable stock mix	**2 tbsp.**	**30 mL**
Whole oregano	**1 tsp.**	**5 mL**
Garlic powder	**1/4 tsp.**	**1 mL**
Salt	**1/2 tsp.**	**2 mL**
Pepper	**1/8 tsp.**	**0.5 mL**
Cayenne pepper	**1/8 tsp.**	**0.5 mL**
Water	**3 cups**	**750 mL**
Garbanzo beans (chick peas), with liquid, puréed in blender	**19 oz.**	**540 mL**
Plain yogurt or sour cream, per serving	**1 tbsp.**	**15 mL**

Heat cooking oil in large saucepan. Add onion. Sauté until soft.

Add next 9 ingredients. Heat, stirring often, until mixture comes to a boil. Boil gently for 15 minutes.

Add garbanzo purée. Stir. Return to a boil. Boil slowly for about 10 minutes to blend flavors well.

Add yogurt to center of each dish. Makes 6 cups (1.5 L).

1 cup (250 mL) contains: *204 Calories (853 kJ); 7.8 g Fat; 7 g Protein; 4 g Fiber*

BLACK BEAN SOUP

Soup at its darkest. Mild and tasty. Easy to double or triple recipe.

Water	**1½ cups**	**375 mL**
Canned black beans, with liquid	**19 oz.**	**540 mL**
Instant vegetable stock mix	**4 tsp.**	**20 mL**
Ground coriander	**¼ tsp.**	**1 mL**
Ground cumin	**¼ tsp.**	**1 mL**
Sweet pickle relish	**1 tsp.**	**5 mL**
Hot pepper sauce (add more if desired)	**¼ tsp.**	**1 mL**
Sour cream	**2 tbsp.**	**30 mL**
Grated Monterey Jack cheese	**2 tsp.**	**10 mL**

Run water and beans through blender. Pour into saucepan.

Add next 5 ingredients. Stir. Heat, stirring often, as mixture comes to a boil. Boil slowly, uncovered, for about 10 minutes to blend flavors.

Pour into 2 bowls. Top each with 1 tbsp. (15 mL) sour cream. Sprinkle each with 1 tsp. (5 mL) cheese. Makes 2 cups (500 mL).

1 cup (250 mL) contains: *338 Calories (1415 kJ); 6.3 g Fat; 19 g Protein; 9 g Fiber*

LENTIL SOUP

Light tan in color. Cooks quicker than most soups. Good light flavor.

Water	**6 cups**	**1.5 L**
Chopped onion	**1⅓ cups**	**325 mL**
Red lentils	**1⅓ cups**	**325 mL**
Chopped celery	**1 cup**	**250 mL**
Salt	**1 tsp.**	**5 mL**
Pepper	**¼ tsp.**	**1 mL**
Garlic powder	**¼ tsp.**	**1 mL**
Instant vegetable stock mix	**2 tbsp.**	**30 mL**
Parsley flakes	**1 tsp.**	**5 mL**
Bay leaf, broken	**1**	**1**
Dried thyme	**¼ tsp.**	**1 mL**

(continued on next page)

Combine first 8 ingredients in large saucepan.

Place parsley flakes, bay leaf and thyme in tea ball or tie in double layer cheesecloth. Add to saucepan. Heat, stirring often, until mixture comes to a boil. Cover. Simmer for about 30 minutes until vegetables are tender. Remove tea ball. Makes 7 cups (1.7 L).

1 cup (250 mL) contains: *170 Calories (710 kJ); 1.5 g Fat; 12 g Protein; 6 g Fiber*

WIENER AND LENTIL SOUP

A thick yummy meal-type soup.

Green lentils	**1 cup**	**250 mL**
Water	**5 cups**	**1.25 L**
Salt	**1/2 tsp.**	**2 mL**
Butter or hard margarine	**2 tbsp.**	**30 mL**
Chopped onion	**2 cups**	**500 mL**
Grated carrot	**1 cup**	**250 mL**
Canned tomatoes with juice, mashed	**28 oz.**	**796 mL**
Bay leaf	**1**	**1**
Garlic powder	**1/2 tsp.**	**2 mL**
Granulated sugar	**1/2 tsp.**	**2 mL**
Salt	**1 tsp.**	**5 mL**
Pepper	**1/4 tsp.**	**1 mL**
Tofu wieners, cut in 1/4 inch (6 mm) slices	**6**	**6**

Cook lentils in water and salt in saucepan for 30 to 40 minutes until tender. Drain. Reserve liquid.

Heat butter in large saucepan. Add onion and carrot. Sauté until soft.

Add tomatoes, bay leaf, garlic powder, sugar, salt and pepper. Simmer for 30 minutes, stirring occasionally.

Add wieners and lentils. Heat through. Add about 2 cups (500 mL) reserved liquid if a thinner consistency is desired. Discard bay leaf. Makes 8 cups (2 L).

1 cup (250 mL) contains: *201 Calories (841 kJ); 3.7 g Fat; 17 g Protein; 6 g Fiber*

BARLEY SOUP

Vegetables at their best.

Water	**6 cups**	**1.5 L**
Instant vegetable stock mix	**2 tbsp.**	**30 mL**
Pearl or pot barley	**1/3 cup**	**75 mL**
Canned tomatoes with juice, cut up	**14 oz.**	**398 mL**
Chopped onion	**1 1/2 cups**	**375 mL**
Chopped celery	**2/3 cup**	**150 mL**
Grated carrot	**1 cup**	**250 mL**
Grated potato	**1 cup**	**250 mL**
Grated yellow turnip	**1/2 cup**	**125 mL**
Soy sauce	**1 tbsp.**	**15 mL**
Salt	**1 tsp.**	**5 mL**
Pepper	**1/4 tsp.**	**1 mL**
Granulated sugar	**1/2 tsp.**	**2 mL**

Chopped parsley or chives, for garnish

Combine first 13 ingredients in large saucepan or Dutch oven. Stir. Heat to boiling. Cover. Boil slowly, for about 1 hour, stirring occasionally.

Garnish with parsley or chives. Makes 8 cups (2 L).

1 cup (250 mL) contains: *98 Calories (412 kJ); 1.3 g Fat; 3 g Protein; 4 g Fiber*

SIMPLE RICE POT

Cheesy rice with tomatoes. Different and satisfying.

Long grain rice, uncooked	**1 cup**	**250 mL**
Canned tomatoes with juice, mashed	**19 oz.**	**540 mL**
Water	**1 cup**	**250 mL**
Granulated sugar	**1 tsp.**	**5 mL**
Salt	**1/2 tsp.**	**2 mL**
Parsley flakes	**1 tsp.**	**5 mL**
Grated medium or sharp Cheddar cheese	**2 cups**	**500 mL**

Combine first 6 ingredients in saucepan. Bring to a boil, stirring often. Cover. Simmer for about 20 minutes until rice is tender.

Add cheese. Stir until cheese melts. Makes 3 1/2 cups (875 mL).

1/2 cup (125 mL) contains: *257 Calories (1077 kJ); 11.7 g Fat; 11 g Protein; 1 g Fiber*

Pictured on page 107.

CAULI-BROC CASSEROLE

This combination has a tomato sauce. Perfect to assemble ahead, then pop in the oven when the time is right.

Butter or hard margarine	**1 tbsp.**	**15 mL**
Chopped onion	**1 cup**	**250 mL**
Canned tomatoes with juice, broken up	**14 oz.**	**398 mL**
Granulated sugar	**1 tbsp.**	**15 mL**
Salt	**1/4 tsp.**	**1 mL**
Pepper	**1/8 tsp.**	**0.5 mL**
Chopped fresh parsley (or 1 tsp., 5 mL, flakes)	**1 tbsp.**	**15 mL**
Dry bread crumbs	**1 1/2 tbsp.**	**25 mL**
Broccoli, 1 bunch, cut up (3/4 lb., 375 g)	**4 cups**	**1 L**
Boiling water		
Cauliflower, cut up (2 1/4 lbs., 1 kg, before trimming)	**5 cups**	**1.25 L**
Boiling water		
Grated medium or sharp Cheddar cheese	**1/2 cup**	**125 mL**
Grated medium or sharp Cheddar cheese	**1/4 cup**	**60 mL**

Melt butter in frying pan. Add onion. Sauté until soft.

Add next 6 ingredients. Stir. Cook slowly for 5 minutes.

Cook broccoli in first amount of boiling water for about 7 minutes until tender-crisp. Drain well. Turn into large bowl.

Cook cauliflower in second amount of boiling water for about 5 minutes until tender-crisp. Drain well. Add to broccoli.

Add first amount of cheese to broccoli and cauliflower. Toss to coat. Place 1/2 in shallow greased 2 quart (2 L) casserole. Pour 1/2 tomato sauce over top. Add second 1/2 vegetables then rest of tomato sauce.

Sprinkle with remaining cheese. Bake, uncovered, in 350°F (175°C) oven for 30 minutes until hot and bubbly. Allow extra time if chilled. Serves 6.

1 serving contains: *156 Calories (653 kJ); 7.6 g Fat; 9 g Protein; 4 g Fiber*

CARROT CASSEROLE

Allow for seconds when you serve this. Delicious.

Large eggs	**3**	**3**
Cooked mashed carrots (cook about 4 cups, 1 L, large dice)	**2 cups**	**500 mL**
Milk	**1 cup**	**250 mL**
Butter or hard margarine, melted	**¼ cup**	**60 mL**
Finely chopped onion	**⅓ cup**	**75 mL**
Salt	**1 tsp.**	**5 mL**
Pepper	**½ tsp.**	**2 mL**
Fine dry bread crumbs	**1 cup**	**250 mL**

Beat eggs in bowl until frothy. Add next 6 ingredients. Mix well.

Add bread crumbs. Stir until blended. Pack into ungreased 2 quart (2 L) casserole. Bake, uncovered, in 350°F (175°C) oven for 1 hour. Serves 8.

1 serving contains: *185 Calories (772 kJ); 9.4 g Fat; 6 g Protein; 2 g Fiber*

DOUBLE SWEET POTATOES

The potatoes are cooked then sliced and placed on a baking sheet, drizzled with sauce and heated in the oven.

Medium sweet potatoes	**2 lbs.**	**900 g**
Boiling water		
Butter or hard margarine	**1 tbsp.**	**15 mL**
Brown sugar, packed	**¼ cup**	**60 mL**
Lemon juice, fresh or bottled	**1½ tsp.**	**7 mL**
Salt	**1/16 tsp.**	**0.5 mL**
Pepper, sprinkle		

Peel sweet potatoes and cook in water until barely tender. Drain. Slice and place on greased baking sheet. Slices should be thicker than for scalloped potatoes.

Melt butter in saucepan. Add sugar, lemon juice and salt. Drizzle over potato slices.

Sprinkle lightly with pepper. Bake in 350°F (175°C) oven for 15 to 20 minutes until hot. Serves 6.

1 serving contains: *211 Calories (885 kJ); 2.4 g Fat; 3 g Protein; 4 g Fiber*

V.G.

SPANISH LENTIL PILAF

Slightly spicy with a chunky look. Very good.

Canned stewed tomatoes	**14 oz.**	**398 mL**
Water	**2 cups**	**500 mL**
Brown rice	**½ cup**	**125 mL**
Green lentils	**¼ cup**	**60 mL**
Red lentils	**¼ cup**	**60 mL**
Chopped onion	**½ cup**	**125 mL**
Chopped celery	**¼ cup**	**60 mL**
Instant vegetable stock mix	**1 tbsp.**	**15 mL**
Dried sweet basil	**1½ tsp.**	**7 mL**
Pepper	**¼ tsp.**	**1 mL**
Grated medium or sharp Cheddar cheese	**1 cup**	**250 mL**

Measure first 10 ingredients into saucepan. Bring to a boil, stirring often. Simmer, covered, until rice and lentils are tender, about 60 minutes.

Add cheese. Stir until it melts. Makes 3½ cups (875 mL).

½ cup (125 mL) contains: *201 Calories (841 kJ); 6.8 g Fat; 10 g Protein; 3 g Fiber*

Pictured on page 71.

PEAS DELUXE

Great taste to this elegant looking dish.

Cooking oil	**1 tbsp.**	**15 mL**
Water	**2 tbsp.**	**30 mL**
Canned small onions in brine, drained (or 2 cups, 500 mL, cooked pearl onions, drained)	**14 oz.**	**398 mL**
Sliced fresh mushrooms	**2 cups**	**500 mL**
Peas, fresh or frozen	**2 cups**	**500 mL**
Salt, sprinkle		
Pepper, sprinkle		

Heat cooking oil and water in frying pan.

Add onions, mushrooms and peas. Sprinkle with salt and pepper. Sauté, covered, stirring often until peas are cooked. Use slotted spoon to remove from pan. Makes 3½ cups (825 mL).

½ cup (125 mL) contains: *76 Calories (317 kJ); 2.3 g Fat; 3 g Protein; 3 g Fiber*

Pictured on page 35.

FRIED RICE

Not fried in the usual manner. The fried part is stirred into the cooked rice. This is an exceptional dish in both appearance and flavor.

Cooking oil	**2 tbsp.**	**30 mL**
Chopped onion	**½ cup**	**125 mL**
Chopped coriander leaves (cilantro)	**1 tbsp.**	**15 mL**
Salt	**1 tsp.**	**5 mL**
Turmeric	**1/16 tsp.**	**0.5 mL**
Basmati rice	**1 cup**	**250 mL**
Water	**2 cups**	**500 mL**

Heat cooking oil in frying pan. Add onion. Sauté until soft and clear.

Add coriander, salt and turmeric. Stir for about 30 seconds. Set aside.

Simmer rice, covered, in water for about 15 minutes until tender and water is absorbed. Stir onion mixture into hot rice. Makes 4 cups (1 L).

***½ cup (125 mL) contains:** 124 Calories (518 kJ); 3.6 g Fat; 2 g Protein; trace Fiber*

1. Biscuits With Herbs, page 44
2. Vegetable Pie, page 104
3. Pinto Tortilla Soup, page 133
4. Minestrone, page 134

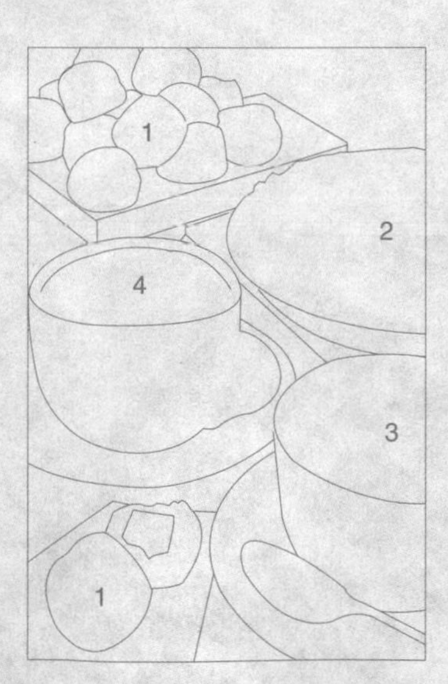

Soup Bowls And Flatware Courtesy Of:
Stokes

Napkins Courtesy Of:
La Cache

PASTA PRIMAVERA

A huge, colorful mixture of pasta and vegetables. Makes a great meal.

Coarsely chopped broccoli	**6 cups**	**1.5 L**
Zucchini, cut in thin fingers	**3 cups**	**750 mL**
Frozen peas	**2 cups**	**500 mL**
Boiling salted water		
Cooking oil	**1 tbsp.**	**15 mL**
Garlic clove, minced	**1**	**1**
Sliced fresh mushrooms	**2 cups**	**500 mL**
Canned tomatoes, drained and broken up	**14 oz.**	**398 mL**
Chopped fresh parsley	**¼ cup**	**60 mL**
PASTA		
Linguini pasta	**1 lb.**	**454 g**
Boiling water	**4 qts.**	**4 L**
Cooking oil (optional)	**1 tbsp.**	**15 mL**
Salt	**1 tbsp.**	**15 mL**
Skim evaporated milk	**13½ oz.**	**385 mL**
Grated Parmesan cheese	**½ cup**	**125 mL**
Salt	**1 tsp.**	**5 mL**
Grated Parmesan cheese, sprinkle		

Cook broccoli, zucchini and peas in boiling salted water in saucepan for 3 minutes until tender-crisp. Drain. Set aside.

Heat cooking oil in wok or frying pan. Add garlic and mushrooms. Sauté until soft and moisture has evaporated.

Add tomatoes and parsley. Sauté for 1 minute. Remove from heat.

Pasta: Cook linguini in boiling water, cooking oil and salt in large uncovered pot for 9 to 11 minutes until tender but firm. Drain. Add to wok. Add vegetables.

Add milk, first amount of Parmesan cheese and salt. Heat and stir until mixture simmers. Simmer for about 3 minutes until it thickens slightly. Turn into large bowl.

Sprinkle with second amount of Parmesan cheese. Makes 13 cups (3.25 L).

1 cup (250 mL) contains: *228 Calories (954 kJ); 3.5 g Fat; 12 g Protein; 4 g Fiber*

Pictured on front cover.

VEGGIE STIR-FRY

Colorful and good. Tofu takes on the flavor of soy sauce.

Soy sauce	**3 tbsp.**	**50 mL**
Sherry (or alcohol-free sherry)	**3 tbsp.**	**50 mL**
Water	**3 tbsp.**	**50 mL**
Garlic powder	**¼ tsp.**	**1 mL**
Ground ginger	**¼ tsp.**	**1 mL**
Cubed or diced firm tofu	**1 cup**	**250 mL**
Cooking oil	**1 tbsp.**	**15 mL**
Large onion, halved lengthwise and thinly sliced	**1**	**1**
Red pepper, seeded and cut in slivers	**1**	**1**
Snow peas, fresh or frozen, thawed	**6 oz.**	**170 g**
Sliced fresh mushrooms	**1½ cups**	**375 mL**
Bean sprouts, 2 large handfuls		
Cherry tomatoes, halved	**8-10**	**8-10**
Cornstarch	**1½ tsp.**	**7 mL**

Combine first 6 ingredients in small bowl. Let stand 1½ hours, stirring occasionally.

Heat cooking oil in wok or large frying pan. Add onion. Stir-fry about 2 to 3 minutes.

Add red pepper and snow peas. Stir-fry about 2 minutes more.

Add mushrooms, bean sprouts and tomatoes. Stir-fry 1 minute. Remove to large bowl. Using slotted spoon, remove tofu to wok. Reserve soy sauce mixture. Add more cooking oil to wok if needed. Stir-fry gently to brown slightly. Add bowl of vegetables. Heat through.

Stir cornstarch into reserved soy sauce mixture. Add to wok. Stir-fry until thickened. Serves 4.

1 serving contains: *200 Calories (835 kJ); 9.7 g Fat; 14 g Protein; 3 g Fiber*

Pictured on page 53.

RISOTTO

Prepare rih-SAW-toh when you have extra time. This Italian speciality requires stock to be added in portions while stirring fairly steadily. A creamy rice dish.

Butter or hard margarine	**2 tbsp.**	**30 mL**
Finely chopped onion	**1 cup**	**250 mL**
Arborio rice (see Note)	**1½ cups**	**375 mL**
Instant vegetable stock mix	**2 tbsp.**	**30 mL**
Boiling water	**5 cups**	**1.25 L**
Red wine (or alcohol-free red wine) or twice as much white wine, (optional)	**2 tbsp.**	**30 mL**
Grated Parmesan cheese	**2 tbsp.**	**30 mL**

Melt butter in heavy saucepan. Add onion. Sauté until soft. Watch that butter doesn't brown.

Add rice. Stir until butter is absorbed without rice getting dry. Be sure to cook slowly.

Stir stock mix into boiling water in separate saucepan. Keep at a simmer. Add 1 cup (250 mL) stock to rice. Stir frequently. When stock is absorbed, add another 1 cup (250 mL) stock. Repeat until all stock has been added. Stir continually until all stock is absorbed. Rice is done when it is creamy, not mushy, and tender but firm. This will take about 25 minutes.

Add wine if using. Stir.

Add cheese. Stir. Remove from heat. Pass extra Parmesan when serving. Makes 4 cups (1 L).

***½ cup (125 mL) contains:** 200 Calories (835 kJ); 4.6 g Fat; 4 g Protein; 1 g Fiber*

Note: Italian Arborio rice is the kind needed for this recipe. If using Canadian or American short grain rice, you may need to add a little more vegetable stock.

SPINACH ROULADE

This green and white roll is a conversation piece to be sure.

ROULADE

Butter or hard margarine	**2 tbsp.**	**30 mL**
Chopped onion	**1½ cups**	**375 mL**
Frozen chopped spinach, thawed and squeezed dry	**2 × 10 oz.**	**2 × 300 g**
Large eggs, room temperature	**4**	**4**
All-purpose flour	**1 cup**	**250 mL**
Baking powder	**2 tsp.**	**10 mL**
Parsley flakes	**1 tsp.**	**5 mL**
Ground nutmeg	**¼ tsp.**	**1 mL**
Salt	**½ tsp.**	**2 mL**
Pepper	**⅛ tsp.**	**0.5 mL**

FILLING

Creamed cottage cheese	**2 cups**	**500 mL**
Chopped chives	**2 tsp.**	**10 mL**
Parsley flakes	**1 tsp.**	**5 mL**
Onion powder	**¼ tsp.**	**1 mL**

Roulade: Melt butter in frying pan. Add onion. Sauté until soft.

Add spinach. Sauté until moisture has evaporated. Cool.

Beat eggs in large bowl until light-colored and thick. Fold in next 6 ingredients carefully. Fold in spinach mixture. Spread in greased wax paper-lined 10 × 15 inch (25 × 38 cm) jelly roll pan. Bake in 400°F (205°C) oven for about 15 minutes until an inserted wooden pick comes out clean. Turn out onto second sheet of waxed paper. Peel off first piece of waxed paper. Roll up roulade with bottom waxed paper, beginning at short end. Cool.

Filling: Stir all 4 ingredients in bowl. Unroll roulade. Spread with filling. Roll up without waxed paper. May be served cold but is much nicer if slices are placed onto greased baking sheet, covered with foil and heated in 425°F (220°C) oven for about 5 minutes until hot. Makes 12 slices.

***1 slice contains:** 142 Calories (594 kJ); 5.6 g Fat; 10 g Protein; 2 g Fiber*

Pictured on page 17.

BRUSSELS SPROUTS SUPREME

A surprise stuffing is hidden in this. An excellent dish. Looks inviting.

Frozen Brussels sprouts	**2 × 10 oz.**	**2 × 284 g**
Finely chopped onion	**1/2 cup**	**125 mL**
Boiling salted water, to cover		
DRESSING		
Dry bread crumbs	**1 1/4 cups**	**300 mL**
Dry onion flakes	**1 tbsp.**	**15 mL**
Parsley flakes	**1 tsp.**	**5 mL**
Poultry seasoning	**1/2 tsp.**	**2 mL**
Salt	**1/4 tsp.**	**1 mL**
Pepper	**1/16 tsp.**	**0.5 mL**
Water	**1/2 cup**	**125 mL**
SAUCE		
Butter or hard margarine	**2 tbsp.**	**30 mL**
All-purpose flour	**3 tbsp.**	**50 mL**
Salt	**1/2 tsp.**	**2 mL**
Pepper	**1/8 tsp.**	**0.5 mL**
Milk	**2 cups**	**500 mL**
Grated Havarti cheese (or Edam or Gouda cheese)	**1/2 cup**	**125 mL**
Ground nutmeg	**1/8 tsp.**	**0.5 mL**
TOPPING		
Grated Havarti cheese (or Edam or Gouda cheese)	**1/2 cup**	**125 mL**

Cook Brussels sprouts and onion in boiling salted water until tender. Drain.

Dressing: Stir first 6 ingredients together in small bowl.

Add water. Mix well.

Sauce: Melt butter in saucepan. Mix in flour, salt and pepper. Stir in milk until mixture boils and thickens.

Add cheese and nutmeg. Stir. Remove from heat. Spread 1/2 Brussels sprouts in greased 2 quart (2 L) casserole. Pour about 1/3 sauce over top. Sprinkle dressing over sauce. Add remaining Brussels sprouts. Pour remaining sauce over top.

Topping: Sprinkle cheese over all. Bake, uncovered, in 350°F (175°C) oven for about 30 minutes until hot. Serves 8.

1 serving contains: *226 Calories (946 kJ); 9.5 g Fat; 11 g Protein; 3 g Fiber*

VEGETABLE SQUARES

A dark base with a creamy souffle-like topping. Contains a variety of vegetables.

BOTTOM LAYER		
Grated cabbage, lightly packed	1 cup	250 mL
Grated carrot, lightly packed	4 cups	1 L
Grated potato, lightly packed	1 cup	250 mL
Instant vegetable stock mix	2 tsp.	10 mL
Boiling water	1 cup	250 mL
Peas, fresh or frozen	1 cup	250 mL
Parsley flakes (or 4 times as much fresh)	1½ tsp.	7 mL
All-purpose flour	2 tbsp.	30 mL
Soy sauce	2 tsp.	10 mL
Salt	1 tsp.	5 mL
Pepper	¼ tsp.	1 mL
Onion powder	½ tsp.	2 mL
Dry bread crumbs	1½ cups	375 mL
SECOND LAYER		
Butter or hard margarine	2 tbsp.	30 mL
All-purpose flour	2 tbsp.	30 mL
Salt	½ tsp.	2 mL
Pepper	⅛ tsp.	0.5 mL
Onion powder	⅛ tsp.	0.5 mL
Plain yogurt	½ cup	125 mL
Large eggs	3	3
Grated medium or sharp Cheddar cheese	¾ cup	175 mL

Bottom Layer: Combine first 5 ingredients in saucepan. Simmer slowly until tender, being careful it doesn't boil dry. Add a little water if needed. Cool slightly. Turn into blender.

Add next 7 ingredients to blender. Purée until smooth. Turn into bowl.

Mix in bread crumbs. Spread in greased 8 × 8 inch (20 × 20 cm) pan.

Second Layer: Melt butter in saucepan. Mix in flour, salt, pepper, and onion powder. Stir in yogurt until mixture boils and thickens. Remove from heat. Cool slightly.

Beat in eggs, 1 at a time. Add cheese. Stir. Pour over bottom layer. Bake, uncovered, in 350°F (175°C) oven for about 40 minutes. Serves 6.

1 serving contains: *388 Calories (1625 kJ); 13.8 g Fat; 16 g Protein; 6 g Fiber*

MEASUREMENT TABLES

Throughout this book measurements are given in Conventional and Metric measure. To compensate for differences between the two measurements due to rounding, a full metric measure is not always used. The cup used is the standard 8 fluid ounce. Temperature is given in degrees Fahrenheit and Celsius. Baking pan measurements are in inches and centimetres as well as quarts and litres. An exact metric conversion is given below as well as the working equivalent (Standard Measure).

OVEN TEMPERATURES

Fahrenheit (°F)	**Celsius** (°C)
175°	80°
200°	95°
225°	110°
250°	120°
275°	140°
300°	150°
325°	160°
350°	175°
375°	190°
400°	205°
425°	220°
450°	230°
475°	240°
500°	260°

SPOONS

Conventional Measure	Metric Exact Conversion Millilitre (mL)	Metric Standard Measure Millilitre (mL)
1/8 teaspoon (tsp.)	0.6 mL	0.5 mL
1/4 teaspoon (tsp.)	1.2 mL	1 mL
1/2 teaspoon (tsp.)	2.4 mL	2 mL
1 teaspoon (tsp.)	4.7 mL	5 mL
2 teaspoons (tsp.)	9.4 mL	10 mL
1 tablespoon (tbsp.)	14.2 mL	15 mL

CUPS

Conventional Measure	Metric Exact Conversion Millilitre (mL)	Metric Standard Measure Millilitre (mL)
1/4 cup (4 tbsp.)	56.8 mL	50 mL
1/3 cup (5 1/3 tbsp.)	75.6 mL	75 mL
1/2 cup (8 tbsp.)	113.7 mL	125 mL
2/3 cup (10 2/3 tbsp.)	151.2 mL	150 mL
3/4 cup (12 tbsp.)	170.5 mL	175 mL
1 cup (16 tbsp.)	227.3 mL	250 mL
4 1/2 cups	1022.9 mL	1000 mL (1 L)

PANS

Conventional Inches	Metric Centimetres
8x8 inch	20x20 cm
9x9 inch	22x22 cm
9x13 inch	22x33 cm
10x15 inch	25x38 cm
11x17 inch	28x43 cm
8x2 inch round	20x5 cm
9x2 inch round	22x5 cm
10x4 1/2 inch tube	25x11 cm
8x4x3 inch loaf	20x10x7 cm
9x5x3 inch loaf	22x12x7 cm

DRY MEASUREMENTS

Conventional Measure Ounces (oz.)	Metric Exact Conversion Grams (g)	Metric Standard Measure Grams (g)
1 oz.	28.3 g	30 g
2 oz.	56.7 g	55 g
3 oz.	85.0 g	85 g
4 oz.	113.4 g	125 g
5 oz.	141.7 g	140 g
6 oz.	170.1 g	170 g
7 oz.	198.4 g	200 g
8 oz.	226.8 g	250 g
16 oz.	453.6 g	500 g
32 oz.	907.2 g	1000 g (1 kg)

CASSEROLES (Canada & Britain)

Standard Size Casserole	Exact Metric Measure
1 qt. (5 cups)	1.13 L
1 1/2 qts. (7 1/2 cups)	1.69 L
2 qts. (10 cups)	2.25 L
2 1/2 qts. (12 1/2 cups)	2.81 L
3 qts. (15 cups)	3.38 L
4 qts. (20 cups)	4.5 L
5 qts. (25 cups)	5.63 L

CASSEROLES (United States)

Standard Size Casserole	Exact Metric Measure
1 qt. (4 cups)	900 mL
1 1/2 qts. (6 cups)	1.35 L
2 qts. (8 cups)	1.8 L
2 1/2 qts. (10 cups)	2.25 L
3 qts. (12 cups)	2.7 L
4 qts. (16 cups)	3.6 L
5 qts. (20 cups)	4.5 L

INDEX

Almond Biscuits 46
Appetizers
  Baked Cheese 19
  Baked Cheese Balls 13
  Black Bean Dip 15
  Cheese Nuggets 19
  Cheese Spread 16
  Chili Con Queso 12
  Falafel 127
  Far East Eggs 11
  Guacamole 14
  Hot Broccoli Dip 10
  Hummus 12
  Quesadilla 95
  Sauced Wieners 10
  Scramble Turnovers 97
  Stuffed Mushrooms 14
Apple Raisin Pancakes 26
Apple Relish 44
Apple Onion Salad 112
Avial 118

Baked Beans, Potluck 92
Baked Cheese 19
Baked Cheese Balls 13
Baked Omelet 25
Barley Soup 138
Bean Bake, Curry 67
Bean Burgers 121
Bean Dip, Black 15
Bean Salad, Overnight 114
Bean Sandwich 117
Bean-Sauced Pasta 65
Bean Sausages, White 76
Bean Soufflé 74
Bean Soup, Black 136
Beans, Potluck Baked 92
Beans, Wieners And 92
Beet Salad 113
Best Roast 81
Beverages
  Chocolate Yogurt Drink 21
  Cranberry Punch 22
  Fruit Shake 21
  Fruity Yogurt Drink 23
  Grapefruit Punch 22
  Orange Yogurt Drink 21
  Peaches And Cream 23
  Pineapple Yogurt Drink 20
  Strawberry Shake 20
  Tofu Shake 20
Biscuits, Almond 46
Biscuits With Herbs 44

Black Bean Dip 15
Black Bean Soup 136
Bran Pancakes, Yogurt 27
Breads
  Almond Biscuits 46
  Biscuits With Herbs 44
  Italian Cheese Bread 45
  Nutty Raisin Bread 47
  Orange Date Loaf 31
  Raisin Wheat Muffins 48
Breakfasts
  Apple Raisin Pancakes 26
  Baked Omelet 25
  Brunch Cake 30
  Cheese-Sauced Eggs 28
  Cheese Strata 24
  Cottage Cheese Pancakes 29
  Eggs On Toast 28
  Fruitier Pancakes 27
  Nutty Fruit Pancakes 27
  Pancake Syrup 23
  Spinach Nests 24
  Tofu Pancakes 29
  Wheat Pancakes 26
  Yogurt Bran Pancakes 27
Broccoli Dip, Hot 10
Broccoli Pasta Casserole 63
Broccoli Rice Bake 61
Brown Gravy 131
Brownies, Graham 41
Brunch Cake 30
Brussels Sprouts Supreme 149
Burgers
  Bean 121
  Meatless 124
  Mushroom 120
  Oatmeal 91
  Protein 119
Burritos 128
Butterscotch Pie 105

Cabbage Salad 117
Cake, Brunch 30
Candy Bar, Nutty 42
Carrot Casserole 140
Cauli-Broc Casserole 139
Cheese, Baked 19
Cheese Balls, Baked 13
Cheese Bread, Italian 45
Cheese Nuggets 19
Cheese-Sauced Eggs 28
Cheese Spread 16
Cheese Strata 24

Cheesecakes
- Pecan Pie ... 109
- Pineapple Cheese Dessert ... 32
- Tofu ... 38

Cheesy Nut Bake ... 85
Cheesy Pasta Casserole ... 69
Cheesy Patties ... 93
Cheesy Rice ... 57
Chick Pea Patties ... 77
Chicken Loaf, Could-Be ... 76
Chili ... 80
Chili Con Queso ... 12
Chocolate Pie ... 105
Chocolate Yogurt Drink ... 21
Chops, Rice ... 88
Chutney, Mango ... 47
Club Sandwich ... 122
Coffee Cakes
- Brunch Cake ... 30

Cookies
- Crispy Peanut Balls ... 42
- Raisin Cookies ... 37

Corn Chip Salad ... 116
Cottage Cheese Pancakes ... 29
Cottage Cheese Squares ... 70
Could-Be Chicken Loaf ... 76
Cranberry Punch ... 22
Crispy Peanut Balls ... 42
Crust, Graham Cracker ... 38
Curry Bean Bake ... 67
Custard ... 41
Cutlets, Vegetable ... 50
Cutlets, Zucchini ... 87

Date Loaf, Orange ... 31
Deep Fruit Pie ... 99
Desserts
- Custard ... 41
- Fruit And Nut ... 34
- Native Pudding ... 40
- Pineapple Cheese ... 32
- Pineapple Crisp ... 39
- Tofu Cheesecake ... 38

Dhal ... 66
Dhal, Zucchini ... 66
Dips
- Black Bean ... 15
- Chili Con Queso ... 12
- Guacamole ... 14
- Hot Broccoli ... 10
- Hummus ... 12
- Spicy Peanut ... 131

Double Sweet Potatoes ... 140
Dressings
- Honey Mustard ... 115
- Island ... 116
- Spicy Peanut ... 131

Easy Lasagne ... 62
Egg Filling ... 129
Eggs, Cheese-Sauced ... 28
Eggs, Far East ... 11
Eggs On Toast ... 28

Fajitas ... 123
Falafel Appetizers ... 127
Falafels ... 127
Falafels, Main ... 127
Fantasy Meatballs ... 84
Far East Eggs ... 11
Favorite Roast ... 82
Filling, Egg ... 129
Fried Rice ... 142
Fruit And Nut Dessert ... 34
Fruit Bars, Zucchini ... 33
Fruit Pancakes, Nutty ... 27
Fruit Pie, Deep ... 99
Fruit Shake ... 21
Fruitier Pancakes ... 27
Fruity Yogurt Drink ... 23

Garbanzo Soup ... 135
Graham Brownies ... 41
Graham Cracker Crust ... 38
Grapefruit Punch ... 22
Gravy, Brown ... 131
Guacamole ... 14

Honey Mustard Dressing ... 115
Hot Broccoli Dip ... 10
Hummus ... 12

Icing, Spicy Nut ... 33
Indian Pudding ... 40
Island Dressing ... 116
Italian Cheese Bread ... 45

Lasagne, Easy ... 62
Lasagne, Lazy ... 56
Lazy Lasagne ... 56
Legume Patties ... 78
Lentil Pilaf, Spanish ... 141
Lentil Soup ... 136
Lentil Soup, Wiener And ... 137

Lentil Stew ... 83
Loaves
  Nutty Raisin Bread ... 47
  Orange Date Loaf ... 31

Macaroni And Cheese ... 64
Main Course Loaves
  Best Roast ... 81
  Could-Be Chicken Loaf ... 76
  Favorite Roast ... 82
  Peanut Loaf ... 49
  Sandwiched Nut Loaf ... 79
Main Falafels ... 127
Mango Chutney ... 47
Meal In A Dish ... 52
"Meat" Scramble ... 96
"Meat" Scramble Pie ... 96
Meatballs
  Fantasy ... 84
  Mock ... 86
Meatless Burgers ... 124
Meatless Moussaka ... 55
Minestrone ... 134
Mock Meatballs ... 86
Moussaka, Meatless ... 55
Muffins, Raisin Wheat ... 48
Mushroom Burgers ... 120
Mushroom Rice Patties ... 86
Mushroom Sauce ... 132
Mushrooms, Stuffed ... 14

Native Pudding ... 40
Noodle Casserole ... 58
Nut Bake, Cheesy ... 85
Nut Dessert, Fruit And ... 34
Nut Icing, Spicy ... 33
Nut Loaf, Sandwiched ... 79
Nutty Candy Bar ... 42
Nutty Fruit Pancakes ... 27
Nutty Raisin Bread ... 47

Oatmeal Burgers ... 91
Oatmeal Patties ... 91
Oatmeal Pie Shell ... 98
Omelet, Baked ... 25
Onion Quiche, Tomato ... 94
Onion Salad, Apple ... 112
Orange Date Loaf ... 31
Orange Yogurt Drink ... 21
Oven Subs ... 120
Overnight Bean Salad ... 94

Pancake Syrup ... 23
Pancakes
  Apple Raisin ... 26
  Cottage Cheese ... 29
  Fruitier ... 27
  Nutty Fruit ... 27
  Tofu ... 29
  Wheat ... 26
  Yogurt Bran ... 27
Pasta
  Bean-Sauced ... 65
  Broccoli Pasta Casserole ... 63
  Cheesy Pasta Casserole ... 69
  Easy Lasagne ... 62
  Macaroni And Cheese ... 64
  Noodle Casserole ... 58
  Sauced ... 60
  Straw And Hay ... 51
Pasta Primavera ... 145
Pasta Salad ... 110
Pasta Veggie Cheese Salad ... 111
Pasta Veggie Salad ... 111
Pasties, Sausage ... 102
Pasties, Veggie ... 102
Pasties, Wiener ... 102
Pastry
  Oatmeal Pie Shell ... 98
  Whole Wheat ... 106
Patties
  Cheesy ... 93
  Chick Pea ... 77
  Legume ... 78
  Falafels ... 127
  Mushroom Rice ... 86
  Oatmeal ... 91
  Rice Chops ... 88
  Saucy ... 68
  Scramble ... 97
  Vegetable Cutlets ... 50
  Zucchini Cutlets ... 87
Peaches And Cream ... 23
Peanut Balls, Crispy ... 42
Peanut Dip, Spicy ... 131
Peanut Dressing, Spicy ... 131
Peanut Loaf ... 49
Peanut Sauce ... 131
Peas Deluxe ... 141
Pecan Pie ... 109
Pecan Squares ... 43
Pie Shell, Oatmeal ... 98
Pies
  Butterscotch ... 105
  Chocolate ... 105
  Deep Fruit ... 99

Pecan ... 109
Tamale ... 103
Vanilla ... 105
Vegetable ... 104
Pilaf, Spanish Lentil ... 141
Pimiento Sauce ... 28
Pineapple Cheese Dessert ... 32
Pineapple Crisp ... 39
Pineapple Yogurt Drink ... 20
Pinto Tortilla Soup ... 133
Pizza ... 100
Pizza Crust ... 100
Pizza, Vegetable ... 98
Potatoes, Double Sweet ... 140
Potluck Baked Beans ... 92
Protein Burgers ... 119
Pudding, Native ... 40
Pumpkin Soup ... 134
Punch, Cranberry ... 22
Punch, Grapefruit ... 22

Quesadilla Appetizers ... 95
Quesadillas ... 95
Quiche
Tomato Onion ... 94
Zucchini ... 101
Quiche Lorne ... 97

Raisin Bread, Nutty ... 47
Raisin Cookies ... 37
Raisin Pancakes, Apple ... 26
Raisin Wheat Muffins ... 48
Red Onion Salsa ... 46
Red Sauce ... 130
Relish, Apple ... 44
Rice Bake, Broccoli ... 61
Rice, Cheesy ... 57
Rice Chops ... 88
Rice, Fried ... 142
Rice Patties, Mushroom ... 86
Rice Pot, Simple ... 138
Rice Veggie Casserole ... 73
Risotto ... 147
Roast, Best ... 81
Roast, Favorite ... 82
Roulade, Spinach ... 148

Salads
Apple Onion ... 112
Beet ... 113
Cabbage ... 117
Corn Chip ... 116
Overnight Bean ... 114
Pasta ... 110
Pasta Veggie ... 111
Pasta Veggie Cheese ... 111
Slivered and Sliced ... 115
Spinach ... 114
Spinach Bacon ... 115
Tabbouleh ... 112
Salsa, Red Onion ... 46
Sandwiched Nut Loaf ... 79
Sandwiches
Bean Burgers ... 121
Bean ... 117
Burritos ... 128
Club ... 122
Egg Filling ... 129
Fajitas ... 123
Falafels ... 127
Meatless Burgers ... 124
Mushroom ... 120
Oven Subs ... 120
Protein Burgers ... 119
Tacos ... 129
Sauced Pasta ... 60
Sauced Wieners ... 10
Sauces
Mushroom ... 132
Peanut ... 131
Pimiento ... 28
Red ... 130
Sweet And Sour ... 132
Tahini ... 130
Tomato Bean ... 65
Tomato Onion ... 68
Saucy Patties ... 68
Sausage Pasties ... 102
Sausages
Tofu ... 74
White Bean ... 76
Scramble, "Meat" ... 96
Scramble Patties ... 97
Scramble Pie, "Meat" ... 96
Scramble Turnovers ... 97
Simple Rice Pot ... 138
Slivered And Sliced Salad ... 115
Soufflé, Bean ... 74
Soups
Barley ... 138
Black Bean ... 136
Garbanzo ... 135
Lentil ... 136
Minestrone ... 134
Pinto Tortilla ... 133
Pumpkin ... 134

Wiener And Lentil ... 137
Spanish Lentil Pilaf ... 141
Spicy Nut Icing ... 33
Spicy Peanut Dip ... 131
Spicy Peanut Dressing ... 131
Spinach Bacon Salad ... 115
Spinach Nests ... 24
Spinach Roulade ... 148
Spinach Salad ... 114
Spreads
Cheese ... 16
Tahini ... 49
Squares
Graham Brownies ... 41
Nutty Candy Bar ... 42
Pecan Squares ... 43
Zucchini Fruit Bars ... 33
Stews
Lentil ... 83
Veggie ... 59
Stir-Fry, Veggie ... 146
Straw And Hay ... 51
Strawberry Shake ... 20
Streusel Topping ... 30
Stuffed Mushrooms ... 14
Subs, Oven ... 120
Sweet And Sour Sauce ... 132
Sweet Potatoes, Double ... 140
Syrup, Pancake ... 23

Tabbouleh ... 112
Tacos ... 129
Tahini ... 49
Tahini Sauce ... 130
Tamale Pie ... 103
Tofu
Best Roast ... 81
Fajitas ... 123
Guacamole ... 14
Sauced Wieners ... 10
Veggie Stir-Fry ... 146
Wiener And Lentil Soup ... 137
Wieners And Beans ... 92
Tofu Cheesecake ... 38
Tofu Pancakes ... 29
Tofu Sausages ... 74
Tofu Shake ... 20
Tomato Bean Sauce ... 65
Tomato Onion Quiche ... 94
Tomato Onion Sauce ... 68
Tortilla Soup, Pinto ... 133
Turnovers, Scramble ... 97
Turnovers, See Pasties

Vanilla Pie ... 105
Vegetable Cutlets ... 50
Vegetable Pie ... 104
Vegetable Pizza ... 98
Vegetable Squares ... 150
Vegetables
Avial ... 118
Brussels Sprouts Supreme ... 149
Carrot Casserole ... 140
Cauli-Broc Casserole ... 139
Double Sweet Potatoes ... 140
Fried Rice ... 142
Meal In A Dish ... 52
Pasta Primavera ... 145
Peas Deluxe ... 141
Risotto ... 147
Simple Rice Pot ... 138
Spanish Lentil Pilaf ... 141
Spinach Roulade ... 148
Zucchini Cutlets ... 87
Zucchini Quiche ... 101
Veggie Casserole, Rice ... 73
Veggie Cheese Salad, Pasta ... 111
Veggie Pasties ... 102
Veggie Salad, Pasta ... 111
Veggie Stew ... 59
Veggie Stir-Fry ... 146
Veggie Wraps ... 75

Wheat Muffins, Raisin ... 48
Wheat Pancakes ... 26
White Bean Sausages ... 76
Whole Wheat Pastry ... 106
Wiener And Lentil Soup ... 137
Wiener Pasties ... 102
Wieners And Beans ... 92
Wieners, Sauced ... 10

Yogurt Bran Pancakes ... 27
Yogurt Drinks
Chocolate ... 21
Fruit Shake ... 21
Fruity ... 23
Orange ... 21
Peaches And Cream ... 23
Pineapple ... 20
Strawberry Shake ... 20

Zucchini Cutlets ... 87
Zucchini Dhal ... 66
Zucchini Fruit Bars ... 33
Zucchini Quiche ... 101

Company's Coming Cookbooks Are Available at Retail Locations Everywhere

MAIL ORDER FORM

Deduct $5.00 for every $35.00 ordered

Save $5.00

ENGLISH

COMPANY'S COMING SERIES

Quantity		Quantity		Quantity	
	150 Delicious Squares		Vegetables		Microwave Cooking
	Casseroles		Main Courses		Preserves
	Muffins & More		Pasta		Light Casseroles
	Salads		Cakes		Chicken, Etc.
	Appetizers		Barbecues		Kids Cooking
	Desserts		Dinners of the World		Fish & Seafood
	Soups & Sandwiches		Lunches		Breads
	Holiday Entertaining		Pies	NEW	Meatless Cooking
	Cookies		Light Recipes	NEW	Cooking For Two (September 1997)

		NO. OF BOOKS		PRICE
FIRST BOOK:	$12.99 + $3.00 shipping = $15.99 each x		=	$
ADDITIONAL BOOKS:	$12.99 + $1.50 shipping = $14.49 each x		=	$

PINT SIZE BOOKS

Quantity		Quantity		Quantity	
	Finger Food		Buffets		Chocolate
	Party Planning		Baking Delights		

		NO. OF BOOKS		PRICE
FIRST BOOK:	$4.99 + $2.00 shipping = $6.99 each x		=	$
ADDITIONAL BOOKS:	$4.99 + $1.00 shipping = $5.99 each x		=	$

FRENCH

JEAN PARÉ LIVRES DE CUISINE

Quantity		Quantity		Quantity	
	150 délicieux carrés		Recettes légères		La cuisine pour les enfants
	Les casseroles		Les salades		Poissons et fruits de mer
	Muffins et plus		La cuisson au micro-ondes		Les pains
	Les dîners		Les pâtes	NEW	La cuisine sans viande
	Les barbecues		Les conserves	NEW	La cuisine pour deux (septembre 1997)
	Les tartes		Les casseroles légères		
	Délices des fêtes		Poulet, etc.		

		NO. OF BOOKS		PRICE
FIRST BOOK:	$12.99 + $3.00 shipping = $15.99 each x		=	$
ADDITIONAL BOOKS:	$12.99 + $1.50 shipping = $14.49 each x		=	$

TOTAL

- **MAKE CHEQUE OR MONEY ORDER PAYABLE TO:** *COMPANY'S COMING PUBLISHING LIMITED*
- **ORDERS OUTSIDE CANADA:** *Must be paid in U.S. funds by cheque or money order drawn on Canadian or U.S. bank.*
- *Prices subject to change without prior notice.*
- *Sorry, no C.O.D.'s*

TOTAL PRICE FOR ALL BOOKS		$
Less $5.00 for every $35.00 ordered	−	$
SUBTOTAL		$
Canadian residents add G.S.T.	+	$
TOTAL AMOUNT ENCLOSED		$

Please complete shipping address on reverse.

Gift Giving

- Let us help you with your gift giving!
- We will send cookbooks directly to the recipients of your choice if you give us their names and addresses.
- Be sure to specify the titles you wish to send to each person.
- If you would like to include your personal note or card, we will be pleased to enclose it with your gift order.
- Company's Coming Cookbooks make excellent gifts. Birthdays, bridal showers, Mother's Day, Father's Day, graduation or any occasion... collect them all!

Shipping address

Send the Company's Coming Cookbooks listed on the reverse side of this coupon, to:

Name: ______________________________

Street: ______________________________

City: ______________ Province/State: ______________

Postal Code/Zip: ______________ Tel: (   )   —

Company's Coming COOKBOOKS

Company's Coming Publishing Limited
Box 8037, Station F
Edmonton, Alberta, Canada T6H 4N9
Tel: (403) 450-6223
Fax: (403) 450-1857

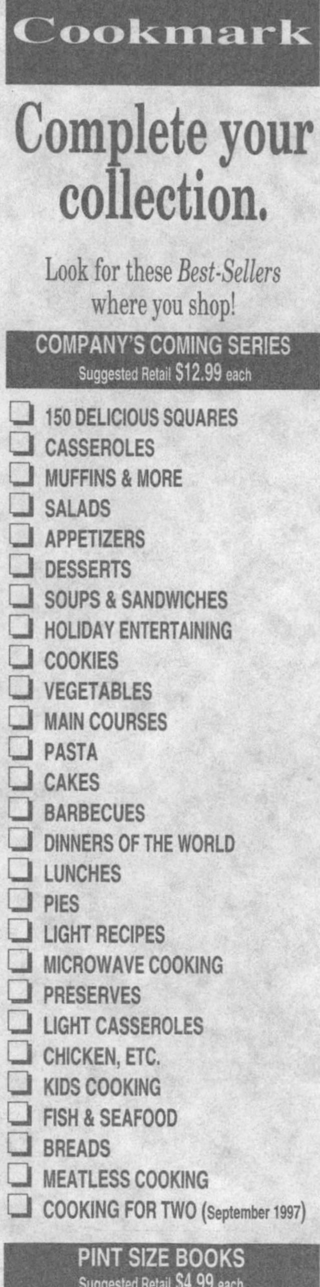

PINT SIZE BOOKS

Suggested Retail $4.99 each

- ❑ FINGER FOOD
- ❑ PARTY PLANNING
- ❑ BUFFETS
- ❑ BAKING DELIGHTS
- ❑ CHOCOLATE

All New Recipes

COQ AU VIN

This excellent variation is out of the ordinary to be sure.

Hard margarine (butter browns too fast)	**1 tbsp.**	**15 mL**
Chicken parts, skin (removed)	**4-5**	**4-5**
All-purpose flour	**¼ cup**	**60 mL**
Sliced onion	**½ cup**	**125 mL**
Canned tomatoes, mashed	**14 oz.**	**398 mL**
Canned whole mushrooms, drained	**10 oz.**	**284 mL**
Bay leaf	**1**	**1**
Garlic powder	**⅛ tsp.**	**0.5 mL**
Granulated sugar	**¼ tsp.**	**1 mL**
Salt, sprinkle		
Pepper, sprinkle		
Red wine (or alcohol-free wine)	**¼ cup**	**60 mL**

Melt margarine in frying pan. Dip chicken in flour. Brown both sides of chicken in frying pan. Transfer to ungreased 1½ quart (1.5 L) casserole.

Add onion to frying pan. Sauté until browned.

Add next 7 ingredients to onion. Stir. Cook slowly for 5 minutes. Discard bay leaf.

Stir in wine. Pour over chicken. Cover. Bake in 325°F (160°C) oven for 1 to 1½ hours until tender. Serves 2.